SMALL BUSINESS BIG MONEY

Financial Success for
Canadian Entrepreneurs

Canadian Cataloguing in Publication Data

Ginsberg, Laurence
  Small business, big money

Includes bibliographical references and index.
ISBN 0-13-897562-0

1. Small business - Finance. I. McDougall,
Bruce, 1950-   . II. Title.

HG4027.7.G56 1997   658.15'92C97-931739-8

© 1997 Larry Ginsberg and Bruce McDougall

Prentice Hall Canada Inc.

Scarborough, Ontario

A Division of Simon & Schuster/A Viacom Company

Prentice-Hall, Inc., Upper Saddle River, New Jersey
Prentice-Hall International (UK) Limited, London
Prentice-Hall of Australia, Pty. Limited, Sydney
Prentice-Hall Hispanoamericana, S.A., Mexico City
Prentice-Hall of India Private Limited, New Delhi
Prentice-Hall of Japan, Inc., Tokyo
Simon & Schuster Southeast Asia Private Limited, Singapore
Editora Prentice-Hall do Brasil, Ltda., Rio de Janeiro

ISBN 0-13-897562-0

Acquisitions Editor: Robert Harris
Copy Editor: Susan Berg
Editorial Assistant: Joan Whitman
Production Coordinator: Julie Preston
Art Direction: Mary Opper
Cover and Interior Design: Gary Beelik

1 2 3 4 5   W   01 00 99 98 97

Printed and bound in Canada

Visit the Prentice Hall Canada Web site! Send us your comments, browse our catalogues,
and more. **www.phcanada.com**

contents

acknowledgments

This book is a collaboration of many people and many lessons learned throughout one's life. I have been blessed twice in my life to work with a great co-author and friend, Bruce McDougall. My thanks to our editors at Prentice Hall who have been great to deal with and very supportive through the whole process. Special thanks to Robert Harris and Karen Alliston. I am grateful for the years of support and encouragement from Professor Rein Peterson, Dean Deszo Horvath, and my colleagues and students of the Schulich School of Business at York University. I work with a great team, including Sandra Verrall, Peter Chambers, David Barrows, and Dave McCarroll. A special thanks to each of them. Thanks to Jim Botterill, Don Johnston, and John Bond for their support throughout. Finally this book could not have been written without the support of my family—my wife Minda and my children Richard, Darrell, and Diana.

Laurence Ginsberg

Larry Ginsberg can be reached through the GinsOrg Web site at **www.ginsorg.com** or by e-mail at **ginsberg@ginsorg.com**. Bruce McDougall can be reached at **bruce@myna.com**.

an entrepreneurial look at money

1

People with a nine-to-five job have no trouble distinguishing between their personal and business finances. They earn their money from their daily labours; their employer hands them a cheque once every week or two or deposits their salary directly into their bank account; then they spend their money on personal necessities and use what's left over to save or spend at their own discretion.

For an entrepreneur, the distinction is not so clear. In fact, any distinction between an entrepreneur's personal and business finances is arbitrary at best; at worst, it's misleading and could guide an entrepreneur toward making the wrong decisions for the wrong reasons. In deciding to start a business in the first place, an entrepreneur makes an intensely personal decision. As we'll see, numerous factors influence that decision, and few of them have anything to do with business.

In fact, your personal goals are inseparable from your business goals. You can't isolate one from the other. You take your accomplishments and your failures personally, whether they happen in business or on the squash court.

It's this factor that makes entrepreneurs unique. Unlike corporate executives, who must put aside their personal likes and dislikes for the sake of the organization, an entrepreneur brings to bear the full force of his personality on his business. As much as any other attributes the business might possess, attitudes distinguish one entrepreneurial business from another.

Every entrepreneurial venture is a unique expression of the owner's personal and business goals. Just as one individual differs from another, every entrepreneurial venture differs from another. Not only do entrepreneurial ventures differ in their goals and aspirations, they also differ in the tools they need to reach them. In particular, the financial tools required to start, nurture, and build an entrepreneurial organization depend on a combination of personal and professional attributes, including the entrepreneur's age, lifestyle, family commitments, personality, experience, values, financial circumstances, and strategies.

Most entrepreneurs use their own financial resources to start their business. Unless they put their money where their mouth is, they'll have difficulty attracting anyone else to invest in their endeavour. From the outset, their personal financial goals and obligations become an inextricable part of their business.

An entrepreneur's business reflects his personality, and his personal goals will determine, to a large extent, the manner in which he runs his business. The more clearly he can articulate the factors that motivate him in his personal life, the more sound the decisions he'll make about building his business.

Personal and business finances become even more inextricably bound as the business evolves. If the entrepreneur remains the sole investor and shareholder, she'll have to decide how to allocate the money that the business generates. If she wants to build the business with the intention of taking it public or selling it, she'll reinvest money that she might, under other circumstances, have distributed to shareholders, including herself. If she feels comfortable with a small, stable, and durable business that generates enough cash to maintain her lifestyle and allows her to spend six weeks a year skiing in Whistler, she'll apply her resources much differently. If she wants to build a business that will endure long after she moves on, she'll have to allocate her financial resources in yet another way, to develop new products and processes, attract new customers, hire new employees, set up new distribution channels, and acquire new technologies. In all cases; though, the entrepreneur's personal goals and aspirations determine the way in which the business applies its resources.

The better you, as an entrepreneur, understand and execute your personal financial strategies, the better you'll run your business. This means that you have to know yourself before you can run your business effectively. You have to know why you want to start a business in the first place and what you want to derive from the business once you get it up and running. The information in the following chapters will help you answer these questions. It will help you coordinate your business and personal objectives and establish the financial priorites you'll need to reach them. Finally, the information will help you make complementary, not contradictory, decisions about your personal and business affairs.

QUALITIES OF AN ENTREPRENEUR

According to academic studies, entrepreneurs share a variety of attributes and qualities. At least one of these qualities involves a willingness to break the mould, to step beyond conventional boundaries and create a new way of doing things. That means, of course, that you can throw all these definitions out the window if you have a good idea and the skill and intelligence to put it into action.

In the meantime, here are some of the personal qualities that you'll commonly find in an entrepreneur.

1. Entrepreneurs are committed and determined to make their ideas work, even if they have to make personal sacrifices.

2. Once an entrepreneur understands what a customer wants, she'll become obsessed with creating value to satisfy the customer's desire.

3. Entrepreneurs can tolerate risk, ambiguity, and uncertainty, but they don't go out of their way to find them. As William Sahlman of the Harvard Business School observes, "One of the greatest myths about entrepreneurs is that they are risk seekers. All sane people want to avoid risk." Entrepreneurs often have to take calculated risks, but they'll do everything they can to minimize their potential impact.

4. Entrepreneurs feel they can rely on themselves to get through a crisis and greet another day. They're creative and they can adapt to changing circumstances. They don't need routine to feel secure. They tend to be unconventional and restless with the status quo, and they have little fear of failure.

5. Entrepreneurs don't crave status or power, but they'll go to great lengths to achieve their personal goals. They can laugh at themselves even though they are under great stress. Surprisingly, despite their intense focus and obsession with success, they work well with other people, who often compensate for the entrepreneur's deficiencies. And entrepreneurs won't stab fellow workers in the back.

6. Entrepreneurs are self-starters and team players. They're not lone wolves. They're patient, experienced, and self-controlled, and they have great integrity. You can rely on an entrepreneur to do what he says.

ENTREPRENEURIAL TRAITS

Entrepreneurs are

- Healthy, energetic, and stable
- Creative and innovative
- Intelligent
- Inspirational
- Decent
- Risk averse
- Adaptive

With all these qualities, entrepreneurs still have strong needs to satisfy, including

1. The need for achievement
2. The need for power
3. The need for affiliation

OWNER/MANAGERS AND ENTREPRENEURS

An owner/manager may buy or inherit a business and feel happy just to let it operate much as it did before she came along. She might know how to manage the business, but she doesn't particularly care if it gets bigger.

Nor will she look for opportunities to expand the business or start a spin-off venture.

An owner/manager will take a conservative approach to making decisions, will evaluate every opportunity before choosing one, and will distinguish between her business and her personal life, keeping each separate from the other.

Nevertheless, the financial decisions that an owner/manager makes about her business determine her ability to meet her personal objectives. She will guide herself according to her personal goals when the time comes to make decisions about her business.

Entrepreneurs, on the other hand, constantly seek new opportunities. They never feel satisfied, and they hate to sit still. If they acquire a business, they'll start looking for ways to make it grow; if they start a business from scratch, they won't feel happy until they've built it into a formidable enterprise. Then perhaps they'll delegate responsibility for managing the company to someone else while they go off and build another one.

Entrepreneurs answer every phone call personally, leap at every opportunity that comes along, make no distinction between their business and their personal lives, and deal with crises as they arise, extinguishing each one the way a fire fighter douses a fire.

Once again, the qualities that drive an entrepreneur will influence the financial decisions she makes about her business and her personal life. By understanding how one affects the other, she can make better decisions about both.

Owner/managers and entrepreneurs all share several qualities. They possess a strong sense of purpose and the intelligence to define their own vision. They will persevere to transform their vision into a practical, revenue-generating operation, whether they want to create a comfortable lifestyle or an empire. They have enough confidence in their own talent that they will reject the financial security of steady employment. But before they take the plunge, they prepare themselves fully. Entrepreneurs may appear to take unnecessary risks, but they usually know exactly what they're doing and how to do it. They've examined the options, the possibilities, the potential rewards, and the potential risks. Once they make a decision to proceed, their faith in themselves sees entrepreneurs through many tribulations that might persuade others to give up.

A QUICK SELF-EVALUATION

Ask yourself these three questions before you go too far in planning your business.

1. Why do you want to start your own business? The answer will help you plan your business according to your personal objectives. You may also find that your reasons for starting a business are not sufficiently serious to motivate you to go further.

2. Does starting a business fit with your attitudes and goals in life? By examining your attitudes and goals, you will also understand how your life as an entrepreneur will contribute to or detract from your personal priorities.

3. What are your strengths and weaknesses? If you know your strengths, you'll see how you can apply them to starting a business. More importantly, by identifying your weaknesses, you can plan to allocate your resources accordingly.

CAN YOU AFFORD TO FAIL?

Once you've identified and evaluated an entrepreneurial opportunity, you have to ask yourself a few questions before you pursue it. Here's one: Can you afford to fail?

Every entrepreneur knows that an endeavour can end in failure. No matter how soundly you plan and how thoroughly you conduct your research, events can take you by surprise and make it impossible to proceed. By the time this occurs, you might have invested a large portion of your own resources, plus the money you've borrowed and raised from other sources. Can you face the consequences if your money and theirs all disappears?

You may not plan to fail, but it could happen. Remain optimistic, plan to succeed, but anticipate failure and do everything you can to avoid it.

If you have a job, for example, you can minimize the risk of failure by remaining on good terms with your current employer. The company may become one of your customers. At the very least, you'll find an open door if your business doesn't succeed and you want to discuss future employment.

You should also invest in your business only as much of your personal savings as you can afford to lose. You wouldn't throw caution to the wind even if your mother asked you to invest in her business. That's not because you don't believe in her abilities, but because you know anything can, and probably will, happen. Wise people don't put all their eggs in one basket, even if they're investing in themselves.

PERSONAL FINANCES COME FIRST

You have to get your own financial house in order before you can persuade anyone else that you can run a business. You might think no one else really matters if you intend to run a one-person operation. But they do. You'll have suppliers who will demand prompt payment. You'll have customers who may or may not pay you on time. As a one-person operation, all these people will have a significant impact on your business and personal finances.

If you intend to build a larger operation, your personal financial affairs play an even larger role in your business affairs, especially in the early stages. You'll have to deal with customers and suppliers, but you'll also have to attract employees and convince potential lenders and investors that they should trust you with their money.

With this in mind, pay your bills promptly, live within your means, and use credit sparingly and wisely. Demonstrate to others that you can handle your own finances and they'll feel confident that you can handle your business finances as well.

WHAT BUSINESS ARE YOU IN?

By the time your business starts growing, you'll face a multitude of challenges that will leave you no time at all for reflection or contemplation. To address these challenges, you'll have to set the appropriate course for your enterprise based on advice that sometimes seems contradictory. Diversify your product line. Stick to what you know best. Retain control of your company. Sell equity to raise capital. Hire a talented leader. Only you can impart the vision of your company. By the time you start sifting through this entrepreneurial medicine chest, it will be too late to go back to the beginning and figure out what business you're in. The more clearly you define your business now, the better off you'll be when you actually start to build it.

The definition will include your competitive strengths so that, as your business grows, you can communicate them clearly to your employees. In a larger organization, attributes like financial controls and reporting relationships have already been established. In an entrepreneurial venture, you have to build them from scratch. Ideally, they should enhance the effectiveness of your organization. To this end, you have to define your goals before you can build an organization that will help you to reach them effectively.

The challenge for the entrepreneur, says Amar Bhide, a professor at the Harvard Business School, lies in distinguishing the critical issues from the minor but nagging problems that confront all businesses as they evolve. These critical issues depend on the entrepreneur's personal goals and aspirations and on the entrepreneur's personal capacity to reach them. "Only when entrepreneurs can say what they want personally from their businesses does it make sense for them to ask the following three questions:

1. What kind of enterprise do I need to build?
2. What risks and sacrifices does such an enterprise demand?
3. Can I accept those risks and sacrifices?

Building Your Enterprise

Entrepreneurs come in an infinite variety of shapes and sizes, with an infinite variety of aspirations. Some want to make a quick profit; others want a lifetime of security. Some want to build a business so that they can sell at a profit and retire; others want to build an empire that will live on long after they die. Some simply can't stand working for anyone else.

Why do you want to start and operate your own business? What are the personal ambitions that a business will fulfill? By answering these questions, you can proceed to define the type of business you want to build. Your personal goals and your personal characteristics have everything to do with the business that you build. They also have a unique impact on the organization's finances.

It's critical that you determine the kind of business you want to start from the outset. The attributes that make self-employment attractive—working hard, applying your talents to a task you enjoy, being self-sufficient, and so on—also limit the potential long-term growth of your business. If you start a personal services company, for example, and discover that you really want to build an empire, you've chosen the wrong type of business to meet your aspirations. In a one-person operation, you'll also have to work hard, continually. You may have to postpone indulging yourself in the lifestyle to which you'd like to become accustomed. It's difficult to combine the demand for long hours in the office with your desire to take a prolonged and relaxing vacation. As one academic says, sole practitioners can't leverage their skills; they can eat only what they kill.

RISKS AND SACRIFICES

Many entrepreneurs want to build a business that will eventually operate without them. They may have talents and skills in abundance, but they don't want the success of their business to depend solely on their personal attributes. However, to build such a business, an entrepreneur has to make a considerable investment over a long period. He has to sacrifice his own personal financial comfort for the sake of his company's growth. He has to reinvest the company's profits, incur personal liabilities, and sell shares of the company to outsiders to raise capital to invest in the business. Throughout this period, the entrepreneur faces the constant risk of failure.

Sole practitioners, on the other hand, can generate an income almost from the moment they begin in business. Depending on no one but themselves, they can make decisions quickly and determine exactly where their next dollar will come from, without consulting anyone else. The financial risk involved in a one-person enterprise is far different, although no less intense, than the risk facing the growing organization. But each entrepreneur will put his organization's finances to far different uses.

As time passes, and if the entrepreneur succeeds, the growing organization stands the chance of accumulating far more equity than the one-person business. But the entrepreneur who builds such a business may have to wait many years before she can enjoy the fruits of her labours.

Meanwhile, the sole practitioner can apply the revenue generated by his business almost immediately to satisfying his personal financial objectives. Few sacrifices are required to generate continuing cash flow. There are no employees to train and pay; no investments required in capital equipment or real estate; no research required into new technologies, processes, or related opportunities. The sacrifices required to stay in business never extend beyond the immediate environment of the sole practitioner himself.

However, a sole practitioner cannot attract and retain skilled employees as readily as the entrepreneur. Nor can he afford to neglect the business for prolonged periods. The money generated by the business depends entirely on the sole practitioner's efforts. When he stops working, the business stops making money.

TOLERANCE FOR RISK

The more clearly you understand your capacity and limitations regarding risk, the more informed your decision about the type of business you want to start and operate. Can you afford to reinvest your organization's profits into the business? For how long? Do other people depend on you to put food on the table? How will they survive while you're depriving yourself for the sake of building your business? Can you afford to risk everything on your business?

STRATEGIES AND TACTICS

Having determined the type of business you want to build, based on the personal factors you perceive in yourself, you can now develop your long-term strategy for building it. "The strategy should integrate the entrepreneur's aspirations with specific long-term policies about the needs the company will serve, its geographic reach, its technological capabilities and other strategic considerations," says Bhide.

You'll naturally develop your strategy based on your vision of your company's long-term future. A strategic investment that makes sense for one company, whose founder intends to build an empire, would make no sense at all for another entrepreneur who simply wanted to maintain her current lifestyle. In both companies, however, a strategy should enable the entrepreneur to make decisions and develop policies that will move the company toward her or his long-term goal.

Your strategy should also enable the business to generate enough income to meet your objectives. If your objective is sustained growth, the company should provide revenues sufficient to invest in expanding the business. If your objective is to maintain your lifestyle, then the business should provide sufficient income for that, as well.

If your business doesn't meet these objectives, then you have to reevaluate your strategy and the factors that might improve the results of your strategic manoeuvres. Can you raise your prices, for example, without alienating customers? Can you increase the productivity of your organization to generate higher returns? Do you have the right number of employees? Are they focusing on the right tasks? Can you allocate your financial resources to more effective ends?

As your business evolves, you'll have to reevaluate your strategies continually. Few businesses can rely on the same strategy tomorrow as they used to reach their position today. New products quickly become old, new ideas obsolete. If you don't plan to sell your organization at its peak, you'll have to analyze the marketplace, identify trends, and develop a revised strategy to accommodate current realities.

If you set out to build a long-term, sustainable enterprise, you'll have to decide where to invest your resources to best enable your business to satisfy your goals. Most businesses start on a shoestring, relying on standard and readily available components, equipment, and processes for most of their operations. As time passes, and if your business is sustainable, you'll inevitably face competitors while responding to changing market demands. To survive, you'll have to decide whether you shoud invest in new employees, new processes, new equipment, new services, or new products. You'll likely have to choose one over the others; few entrepreneurs can afford to choose them all.

Finally, you'll have to determine the rate at which your organization grows. This, too, will depend to a large extent on your personal ambitions. The faster your organization grows, the more intense the growing pains. How much stress and anxiety can you tolerate?

GROWTH DEPENDS ON FINANCING

The rate at which your organization grows will also depend on available financing. Most new ventures have little money in reserve; most goes toward building and sustaining growth. The amount of money your business generates will determine the rate at which it grows. The personal aspirations that you identified at the outset will now influence the financial constraints on your business. If they don't correspond—if you change your mind or fail to understand your aspirations in the first place—you'll grow increasingly frustrated with the financial restrictions that keep your organization from expanding more quickly.

GROWTH AND CASH FLOW

A conventional formula says that a self-funded business tends to have its expansion limited by the rate at which it can generate cash flow. Rapid cash flow offers rapid growth possibilities. The inverse is also true.

Along with your own leadership, as well as teamwork and capabilities within the organization, your access to funding will determine the success of your business. If you know at the outset that you want to build your business beyond a small, steady operation, you'll put the mechanisms in place that will give you access to a variety of financial resources.

Rapid growth can sometimes present as many challenges as no growth at all. Systems, employees, and distribution all have to be realigned to accommodate the increased activity. Without one, the others will not perform adequately, and the whole enterprise may topple. As the organization's leader, you have to articulate your goals and strategies and communicate them effectively to your employees, so that everyone pulls together to meet the organization's objectives. Meanwhile, unless you operate a small and sustainable enterprise, your own role within the organization will change. Are you willing to stand back and let others do the work that you initially did yourself? Will all the fun go out of your life if you have to delegate tasks? Can you teach other people to do your job? More importantly, can you trust them to do it well, even if they don't do it in the same way as you do?

AUTONOMY AND CONTROL

As a business grows, the entrepreneur has to find the proper balance between autonomy and control. To perform well, employees have to feel free to apply their talents and skills. At the same time, you have to feel reassured that your financial house is in order. How do you give employees the freedom to make decisions and initiate ideas while maintaining tight control over the organization's finances?

When you start answering such questions, you'll likely have to invest in technology that will enable you to monitor your organization's finances while tracking future funding requirements. Record-keeping and controls will not only keep your business operating effectively, they will reassure lenders, investors, and potential purchasers that your business is sound.

The resolution of all these issues depends to a large extent on your own personal goals. By evaluating your personal objectives, aspirations, and dreams while determining the type of business you want to build, you can resolve the issues effectively. At the same time, you'll avoid disrupting the lives of the people who depend on you: your family, your customers, your employees, your investors, your creditors, your suppliers, and yourself.

We will deal with personal finance in Chapters 2 through 4, and with business planning in Chapters 6 through 8. Chapters 9 and 10 combine the two. There are four appendices to assist you. Appendix 1 highlights some web sites that you may want to visit for advice (there are many more; this is just a sample). Appendix 2 is a blank set of personal financial planning forms for your use. Appendix 3 and 4 are examples, respectively, of a personal financial plan and the financial content of a business plan.

organizing your financial life

2

Just because you make a lot of money, you're not necessarily rich. You don't become truly rich until your money starts working for you. The better you make your money work for you, the less you have to work for your money. When you don't have to work for your money, you can turn your attention and energy to more interesting goals, such as building your business and creating a life.

The state of mind that keeps you focused on building a business will also help you keep your financial life in order. By keeping the risks and rewards in perspective, by recognizing the obstacles without letting them intimidate you, by approaching your financial planning as a potential opportunity rather than an unequivocal penalty, you can take the steps required to accumulate wealth. What you do with it depends on your personal goals and ambitions.

Your state of mind determines your potential success in financial planning as in life in general. With a negative attitude, people sabotage themselves before they even get started. Financial planner Michael Reardon calls this "No Chance Financial Planning." He says, "If you keep on doing what you've always been doing, you're going to keep on getting what you've always been getting."

Despite what you've heard, money is not the root of all evil. The absence of money creates far more problems than its presence. As an entrepreneur, you probably already know this. But even entrepreneurs often feel reluctant to admit that they like money, that they want more of it, and that they're working hard to get it. This reluctance causes problems of its own. Instead of analyzing the ways in which money works and determining how we can make money work for us, we feign disinterest in the topic altogether.

In fact, few people really want money for its own sake. No one takes a bath in, or papers the walls of his condo with, dollar bills. What we really want, if we only took the time to realize it, is prosperity, comfort, and financial independence. Seen from this perspective, money is a social nutrient. Applied properly, with discretion and wisdom, money enhances our lives.

To accumulate money, however, we have to stop spending everything we have. We have to take what we have and invest it in a way that will create more. As Reardon says, we have to think rich. Rich people say, "How can I invest this money today in a way that will guarantee my financial abundance tomorrow?" The rest of us say, "Charge it!" When rich people come into a large sum of money, their first thought is how to double or triple the money. When the rest of us come into a large sum of money, our first thought is how we can spend it.

WHY PLAN?

The better we organize our personal finances, the more time, energy, and clear thinking we can devote to our businesses. Contrary to some opinions, no one works well under sustained pressure. If we can reduce the financial pressure in our personal lives, we'll have more capacity to cope with the inevitable pressures of building a business.

START INVESTING NOW

Many factors will determine your approach to financial planning. In addition to your own personality, you also have to consider your age, education, experience, family status, and health. You have to determine how you want to live your life, and how you will coordinate your personal life with your business. You'll have to decide whether you want to make financial sacrifices now for the sake of the future growth of your business or reward yourself now while maintaining your business as it currently operates.

Regardless of our particular personality and ambition, all of us have to realize that we can afford to follow a financial plan, no matter how much or how little money we have to begin with.

Most people think that if they can't afford to save 10%, then there's no point in saving anything at all. Nothing could be further from the truth. If you can save 10% of your money, that's above average. If you can save 5%, that's still a beginning. Any amount will do. You may think you don't have enough to start investing. But in fact, you don't have enough money not to start investing. If you save just $3.25 a day—the price of two coffees, a doughnut, and a newspaper—think about this:

- $3.25 a day adds up to about $100 a month.
- In 10 years you'll have $19,000.
- In 20 years you'll have $57,000.
- In 25 years you'll have $98,000, assuming a 10% annual return on your money.

Saving money to invest has to become one of our first priorities, not a reward we can look forward to collecting at some future date. Even if we invest only $3.25 a day, we have to do it as faithfully and predictably as we eat. The day we put saving money at the top of our list of "must-do" activities, we'll begin our journey toward financial abundance.

PLAN YOUR WORK AND WORK YOUR PLAN

How do you develop an effective investment plan? You start by setting realistic financial goals. That means identifying your goals for the short term, the intermediate term, and the long term. How much wealth do you want to accumulate this year? Over the next five years? Over the next 10 and 20 years? What's your lifetime financial goal?

The answers to these questions will have a major influence on the way you build your business. If you have no family and no ambition to accumulate a great deal of money in a short period, you'll have different priorities from those you'd have if you needed money to support three children and intended to retire at the age of 45.

Planning your personal and your business future simply takes a little imagination. You have to understand clearly why you want to become financially independent. Once you know the whys, the how to's will take care of themselves.

DON'T PLAN TO SAVE, PLAN TO SPEND

To invest successfully, you have to start paying attention to where your money goes. Forget about budgeting. For most people, budgets just don't work. What you really need is a spending plan.

You need to figure out, in advance, how much money you'll spend in each category of your life, so that you'll always have the money you need.

DEVELOPING AN INVESTMENT PHILOSOPHY

You've attained financial independence when your money generates enough interest to live at your current lifestyle (or better) for the rest of your life, without ever having to work again unless you want to. For some of us, that means $50,000 a year. For others, it means $25,000 or $100,000. Each of us has to figure out an ideal amount.

Let's assume that $50,000 a year will do the trick. If you can earn an 8% return on your money, you'll need to accumulate about $625,000 of interest-earning capital. That may seem like a lot now. But it's well within your reach, even if you have only a small amount to invest.

Your personal investment philosophy will determine how you handle the future ups and downs that inevitably occur in financial markets. It will also determine how you run your business in the short, intermediate, and long term.

Your investment philosophy will influence your investment decisions, and those decisions will shape your financial destiny in your personal and business life. Ideally, you'll develop a philosophy that encourages you to learn from your mistakes, change your approach, and then get back up to bat so that you can take another cut at the ball.

RISK AND EMOTION

As we've mentioned before, entrepreneurs do not take unnecessary risks. In conducting your personal and business financial affairs, you want to minimize risk and maximize rewards.

Nevertheless, for most people, including entrepreneurs, investing in anything but their own businesses remains a very emotional affair. The more risk involved, the more emotional it becomes. Unfortunately, emotion and objectivity are inversely related: The more emotional you become, the less objective you can be.

In defining your personal and business financial strategy, you have to determine how much risk you can tolerate. Then you can organize your finances with investments that correspond to your risk threshold.

How do you know where your threshold lies? Here's a good rule of thumb: If you can't concentrate on your business, sleep at night, or stop worrying about your investments, then you've probably exceeded your risk threshold. If you can't think of opening the stock pages tomorrow without salivating, then you're too emotionally involved.

You have to be selective in choosing your investments. Many people jump into the first investment that comes along without considering the risk involved. Only after they start losing money do they think about how they could have acted differently.

NO RISK, NO REWARD

You may not want to lose sleep over your investments or listen to your stomach churning as you sit on the bus reading the stock pages. But if you can't accept a little risk, you'll never accumulate many rewards. If you can't tolerate any more risk than you find in a Canada Savings Bond (CSB), then you've got a problem. Your money will not be working to its full potential. You'll have to settle for doubling your money every twelve to fourteen years, when you could be doubling it every four to six years.

There's nothing wrong with a few low-risk investments. Every portfolio should have some, especially as you get older. If your more aggressive investments under-perform your expectations, those low-risk investments will still provide you with some economic security.

Some investments, however, can earn you 20% to 40% or more annually. But they come with a slightly higher risk of losing your money.

Regardless of the riskiness of your investments, you should always educate yourself about a potential investment before you buy. People who invest on impulse become nervous wrecks, usually poor ones. Financial planning is supposed to free you from the torment of anxiety while gaining you some financial freedom. You don't want to risk your emotional health for an uncertain financial future.

Buy Value, Not Hype

One of the basic rules of successful money management is: never buy stock, invest only in companies. If your brother-in-law gives you a typical hot tip about a sure thing that can't possibly fail, he may be right and he may be wrong. You'll never know unless you find out more about the company, from someone other than your brother-in-law.

In the meantime, if you're the last person on the deal team, you can rest assured that the big money has already been made. The price that you pay is probably a lot more than the company's actually worth.

In fact, nine times out of ten, by the time you read about a stock in *The Globe and Mail* or elsewhere in the news, you'll end up paying retail when you buy it. And when it comes to investments, the retail price is too much. You want to buy below retail. You want to buy wholesale. That way, you can get some real value for your money.

LOOK TO THE FUTURE

Forget the hype and focus on the facts. When your only reason for buying an investment is a quick buck, you'll get caught up in the emotion of the moment, rather than thinking about long-term growth over a lifetime.

Before you buy any investment, develop a list of criteria that the investment must meet before you part with any of your money.

In addition, make sure that you feel emotionally comfortable with your decision. If all you do is make money from your investment, that's fine. But if you really believe in your investment and can have fun at the same time, then you'll come out a winner no matter what happens.

HOME IS WHERE THE HEART IS—AND WHERE THE BRAIN IS

People tend to use their good judgment when they buy a house more often than they use it in making any other potential investment. They take all the right steps.

First, they define what they really want. They set goals, and they list the criteria that must be met before they'll take action. They say, "What we need is a three-bedroom, two-bathroom house, with a modern kitchen and large backyard. It must be close to a school in a safe neighbourhood, and we're not paying a dime more than $200,000."

Second, they usually hire real-estate experts. They'll pay an inspector to check the property for any structural flaws and defects. They'll hire a lawyer to check the contract to make sure that all the terms of the agreement are in order. They'll arrange financing through a lender who knows how to structure a mortgage loan, and they'll work to get the best deal possible.

Third, they must feel emotionally comfortable with the house before they buy it. They know that, no matter what happens in the real-estate market over the short term, they'll enjoy living in their house. They're not just paying the price, they're enjoying it. The thought of buying today and selling tomorrow is out of the question.

Fourth, they buy and hold for the long term. The people who lose money in real estate are the ones who see everyone else making money and then decide to jump on the bandwagon to make a quick buck by flipping their property. That's impulsive, not smart, and it's a big mistake.

GET RICH QUICK VERSUS GET RICH

In making other types of investments, however, most of us bring the same fast-paced expectations as we bring to our careers: go, go, go, hurry, hurry, hurry. With investments, that's a big mistake. The faster you try to make money from investments, the more likely it is you'll lose it. Of all people, an entrepreneur should understand how hard it is to succeed with a business venture and how long it takes to build a business. Entrepreneurs know that there's no such thing as a sure-fire get-rich-quick scheme. As an entrepreneur, you wouldn't try to build a business overnight; nor should you invest your money that quickly.

Building wealth is a long-term process. You have to apply the same long-term attitude to the process as you bring to your business. Patience and discipline are the words to live by, in your personal and business affairs alike.

THINK LONG TERM AND DON'T FOLLOW THE HERD

If you look at the top money managers over the past 20 years—people like John Templeton and Warren Buffett—you'll find that they were rarely number one over the short term. On many occasions, they actually lagged behind the competition. But over the long term, the Templetons and the Buffetts beat the pants off the rest of the crowd.

How can that be? Every single year they followed the same long-term strategy, the same tried-and-true principles. Some years were up, and some years were down, but the profits continued to grow, year by year. At the end of the day, when the tally was taken, these long-term money managers had earnings three to four times as great as the market average.

The most successful money managers also take a contrarian approach to investing. That means when a majority of people jumps on the bandwagon, they jump off. Or, when the majority jumps off, they jump on.

The basic premise is that the majority is always wrong. That may sound undemocratic, but in financial markets at least, it happens to be true.

If you want to be a successful investor, you have to find real value when nobody else wants it; then, when everybody else wants it, sell it to them and take your money. That's how John Templeton did it, investing not only his money but other people's as well. Time and again he has said that he owes his success to buying companies that have real value when they're unpopular and selling them when they become popular. Like all good investors, he invests in companies, not in stocks.

NEVER BUY OUT OF GREED AND SELL OUT OF FEAR

After a successful market rally, many investors become greedy. Once you become greedy, the party's over.

The greedier you become, the more emotional you become. In fact, greed is one of the seven deadly sins because it violates our own self-governance and places us at the mercy of a passion beyond our control. The more emotional you become, the less objective you become. The less objective you become, the faster your money will slip out of your hands into somebody else's.

The best antidote to greed is a good dose of patience and discipline. Patience and discipline may not get the blood pumping and the adrenaline flowing, but they allow us to maintain an even pace. An even pace is crucial to building wealth.

If something is a good investment today, it's probably going to be a good investment tomorrow. It's the people who think they've got to buy it now who usually sell first, out of fear, and buy last, out of greed.

The classic example: the stock-market crash of October 1987. Did everybody lose money when the market crashed? Of course not. Did some people actually make money? Yes. Who were the biggest losers? The ones who bought late in the game and paid over-inflated prices. When the crash was over, stocks that were previously selling at retail were selling at wholesale prices.

Did the people who bought real value prior to the crash lose money when the market tumbled? No. People who maintained their long-term investment philosophy didn't lose money. They suffered some temporary paper losses. But within a short while, the stock market rebounded, and they recovered all their previous losses.

THE RISKS OF INVESTING

As an entrepreneur you'll eventually have to start raising money. (We'll
deal with this later in the book.) You'll ask people to take a risk that you'll
take their money and make it grow.

As an investor, you're on the other side of the equation. You have to decide how much money you want to invest, the amount of risk you want
to incur, and the return you expect from your investment.

Even the most daring entrepreneur (and there aren't many of them
around; they don't last long) often feels reluctant to risk his own money
on an investment less conservative than a safe bank account.

There's an old saying: We all want to go to heaven, but none of us wants
to die. We take the same attitude when it comes to investing. We all want
to double our money, but none of us wants to take a financial risk.

But if you didn't take any risks at all, you'd never get out of bed in the
morning. You certainly wouldn't start your own business. Life is a risk.

Here's an example: Stock-car racing is inherently risky. There's always
the risk that you'll drive into a wall at 150 km/h, roll over three times, and
ride your crankshaft into the sunset.

But stock-car drivers understand the risks involved in their sport. And
within this context, they don't take chances. Unlike many drivers on the
less risky but more dangerous highways of our nation, they think about
what they're doing. And most of the time, they do it without killing themselves. In the midst of all that risk, they actually drive safely.

When it comes to our financial security, we operate within a general context of risk. There's political risk, for example, and interest-rate risk, and currency risk. These risks affect us even if we keep our money in a sock in the basement. But within the context of these risks, a good investor, like a good driver, can operate safely.

THERE'S NO SURE THING

No investment is risk free. Our opportunity for gain is always balanced by our risk of loss. But we can calculate our risk. When we do, we can see that an investment in a stock or mutual fund presents far less risk of losing money than an investment in a lottery ticket. Yet which investment attracts more investors?

We have to learn how to master risk, not become its slave. People who measured their risk and acted on it made a fortune during the crashes of 1929 and 1987. Likewise, investors who financed real-estate deals prior to the German hyperinflation of 1923 ended up paying off their properties with pennies on the dollar. Not all of them were just lucky.

Investors who understand risk can make a profit, whether the market goes up or down.

The greater the risk, the greater the potential reward. But we have to determine our tolerance for risk, in our personal lives and our business affairs. To do that, we have to recognize the different types of risk that we encounter as we invest. Not all risks present themselves in the same manner. Like a convention of scary monsters, each one has its own schtick. Some of them eat you quickly. Others like to suck the juices out of you slowly and agonizingly. Still others sneak up behind you and smother you, and some fall on you from a great height.

PURCHASING POWER RISK

If you stuff your money in a sock and bury it in the ground, it will lose its value. At an average inflation rate of 4% a year, the cost of living doubles every 18 years.

To avoid it, most Canadians put their money in a government-insured, Guaranteed Investment Certificate (GIC). These provide a fixed rate of return. They're predictable and safe. But they're not entirely risk free. If you invest $10,000 in a GIC that pays 6%, when inflation is running at 4%, you end up with a 2% return.

At 2% a year, you'll double your money every 36 years. In three centuries, you'll be able to afford a bigger house. Meanwhile, if inflation rises to 7%, you'll actually lose 1% of the value of your investment every year.

Investments that provide a variable rate of return, such as common stocks and real estate, usually respond positively to inflation and let you stay ahead of the game.

INTEREST-RATE RISK

When inflation slows down, interest rates fall. If your fixed-interest investment such as a GIC or CSB matures at this point, and you reinvest it, you'll have to take a cut in your rate of return. During 1981 and 1982 the rate of interest on CSBs fell almost overnight from 19.5% to 10.5%. People like senior citizens, who derived their fixed income from their investments in CSBs, found their incomes cut in half.

To protect yourself against interest-rate risk, you should keep some of your money in short-term investments, like a money market fund, so you'll have the cash on hand to invest when rates start to rise again.

POLITICAL RISK

When a nation becomes politically unstable, the value of investments in the nation goes down. That's because the risk of turmoil, revolution, disintegration of the country, radical changes in tax policy, and other potential crises becomes greater. In March 1994, for example, the leading candidate for the Mexican presidency, Luis Colosio, was assassinated. In the following two weeks the Mexican stock market fell 10%. In 1939 German troops marched through Czechoslovakia. Stock prices around the world fell 20%. In 1974 the Watergate scandal contributed to a stock-market tumble of 28%.

For investors who understand the nature of political risk, these unpredictable occurrences present excellent buying opportunities.

CURRENCY RISK

When the value of the dollar falls from US89¢ to US70¢ in two years, we've just experienced the effects of currency risk. When we hand a bank teller a crisp new Canadian $100 bill and get back $65 in ugly wrinkled U.S. dollars, currency risk has descended upon us again. When you invest in Greece, and the Greek drachma suddenly loses its value because some general has threatened to occupy the Parthenon, you get creamed when you sell your investment and convert the proceeds back into Canadian dollars. There are ways to protect yourself against currency risk, which we'll discuss later. For now, you should recognize the risk.

TAX RISK

If you invest outside an RRSP or a RRIF, you'll have to share your capital gains, interest earnings, and dividends with Revenue Canada. The tax is calculated differently on each kind of investment income. Your marginal tax rate plays a role, too. But you can arrange your investments so that you pay the least amount of tax possible.

If you pay yourself a salary of $40,000 a year, for example, and you earn $1,000 in interest from a CSB, $1,000 in capital gains from your stock mutual fund, and $1,000 in dividends from preferred stocks, all held outside your RRSP or RRIF, here's approximately what you'll have to pay in tax:

- CSB interest: $1,000 × 42% = $420
- Mutual fund capital gain: $1,000 × 31% = $310
- Stock dividends: $1,000 × 25% = $250

As you can see, the best tax treatment comes from dividends, followed by capital gains and then interest income.

In the example above, your $1,000 in interest from a CSB turns into $580 after taxes. With inflation, that $580 will likely lose even more value. Also, your fixed-income investment is locked in for up to five years. But the tax rate keeps changing in the meantime. If you increase your salary, for example, you enter a higher tax bracket. The government can simply raise taxes. All this reduces your income from your fixed-rate investment even further.

Dividends work differently. Say you bought shares in a stock mutual fund for $10 a share, outside of your RRSP or RRIF, and the stock market went down. If you then sold those shares a year later for $7 each, you'd take a capital loss of $3 a share. You can use capital losses for tax purposes to offset taxable capital gains. So even a loss on the stock market is tempered by potential tax benefits.

Ultimately, of course, you have to learn enough to make your own decisions about your investment plan.

UPS AND DOWNS

Between 1946 and 1990, the stock market declined significantly 14 times. Those periods of decline lasted from a few months to two years. The biggest drop occurred over a 23-month period from January 1973 to December 1974, when the Dow fell 45%.

Despite those 14 major declines, you would have made money in the market if you'd held on to your investments, even if you bought them at their peak. The last four major peaks in the market occurred in 1969-70, 1973-74, 1981-82, and 1987. If you'd invested $5,000 at each of those market peaks, your $20,000 total investment would have grown to $150,000 by 1994. Considering that you'd invested during the worst possible times over the past quarter century, that's not bad.

Over the short term, however, investors in the stock market will most likely lose. That's because stock-market investing is not a short-term activity. Over the long term, a stock will usually perform just as an investor expects it to. But it won't perform at the expected times. Because of this, you will likely purchase a stock only to see it start dropping in value. Two weeks later, as the stock continues its death-defying nose-dive into oblivion, you'll be tempted to sell out of fear, having lost a good portion of your original investment. If you respond to your fear, the stock will start to rise again, shortly after you sell it.

You have to be prepared to ride out the ups and downs. Invest for the long term and forget about the short-term fluctuations.

HIGH-RISK AND LOW-RISK INVESTMENTS

The following investments are ranked in descending order, according to their degree of risk:

- Commodities
- Currencies
- Options

- Precious metals
- Common stocks
- Preferred stocks
- Bonds
- Mutual funds
- Money market funds
- GICs
- Bank savings accounts
- Canada Savings Bonds
- Treasury bills

THE SPENDING PLAN

We'll explain in a moment how budgets work. But you should know from the outset that budgets alone usually don't work as a way to accumulate wealth. Just like a diet that tells us what we can and can't eat, a budget simply tells us what we can't afford. It doesn't keep us from buying it.

If you really want to develop the wealth-building mentality, you should stop thinking in terms of budgeting and start thinking in terms of spending. Instead of a budget, develop a spending plan. You'll still buy what you were buying before, but you'll spend less. And the less money you spend, the more you'll have to invest.

THE BUDGET

Your budget, like your business, will reflect your own personality. If you like details, you'll keep track of every penny you spend, earn, and invest. If you like to delegate, you'll leave the saving, investing, and spending to someone else, using pre-authorized debits, RRSP deductions, and other mechanisms. The importance of the budget lies in the planning.

Your budget will reflect your lifestyle, your financial goals, and your spending habits. It will also reflect your age, marital status, family situation, and current financial condition. The importance of all these details extends beyond the budget itself. They also influence the decisions you make about your business, your capacity to raise money, and your tolerance for risk.

In preparing a budget, you should calculate
- Your net worth,
- Your personal and business financial objectives,
- Your total household income, and
- Your spending habits.

NET WORTH

By calculating your net worth, you can determine the amount by which your total assets exceeds your total liabilities. You can then make informed decisions about the amount you can invest in your business, the amount you can devote to personal expenses, and the flexibility you have in shifting money from one area to the other. You will know, for example, if you can afford a new car or whether you should pay off your credit card.

YOUR FINANCIAL OBJECTIVES

You've already identified at least one of your financial objectives: You want to build a business. Along with your other financial goals, this will determine your budget and the decisions you make about spending in your personal and business life. Your budget should accommodate your other financial goals as well—over the short term and long term.

In the short term, for example, you may want to buy a car or a house or go on vacation. Over the longer term, you'll want to save money for your family's future—education for the children, for example, and your own retirement. You may be tempted to sacrifice your long-term goals for the sake of your immediate business needs. Money you might ordinarily set aside for your RRSP, you might instead invest in your business. This would be a mistake. We've already emphasized the importance of putting your financial eggs in different baskets. Retirement is one long-term financial basket that you shouldn't ignore, for your own sake and the sake of the people who depend on you.

In defining your goals, you have to determine where you want to be in five years, ten years, and even further into the future. You don't have to be overly specific. But you have to form some clear goals for the future before you can assess whether you can achieve them. If you have $10,000 in RRSPs and you want to retire at the age of 55 with an annual income equivalent to $55,000 a year, you can determine how much you have to set aside every year to reach your goal. If the amount seems unrealistic, you have to revise your goal or figure out another way to reach it.

In setting your budget, don't forget about emergencies. They happen, and even the smallest emergency such as an illness or a family situation that keeps you away from your business can cost money.

Your budget should include your household income, including the income of your spouse and your children, social security benefits, interest, dividends, and other payments. Your own income will be more difficult to determine, since it depends on the success of your business. By calculating how much you need to pay for annual RRSP contributions, taxes, mortgage payments, and other expenses, however, you can determine the minimum amount of personal income you'll need to generate from your business.

SPENDING PLAN

As part of your budget, you have to determine how much you have to spend every month. This figure will include fixed costs such as mortgage payments, taxes, car payments, insurance, clothing, food, and other essentials. It will also include incidentals and discretionary spending such as vacations, restaurant meals, magazines and newspapers, and CDs. To make sure your spending plan accommodates your family, you should discuss these expenditures with your spouse and your children so that everyone knows how they fit into the big picture.

Your credit card receipts, cancelled cheques, income tax statements, and utility bills will help determine your spending plan. The more clearly you can define your spending patterns, the better you can develop your plan. If necessary, you can look for expenses to modify, thereby reducing your total expenditures.

BUDGET IN A NUTSHELL

You can now calculate your budget based on your net worth, your personal and business financial objectives, your estimated net income, and your spending plan.

You know how much you have to spend on fixed expenses such as mortgage, taxes, and utilities. You also know how much you spend on incidentals and frills. You know, too, how much you want to invest in your own business and how much you want to set aside for your retirement. To meet these expenses, you can now determine how much your business has to generate so you can pay yourself an adequate income.

If your income and expenses seem to conflict, you can determine how to adjust them accordingly. Can you reduce your expenses? Can you increase your income? Can you defer major expenditures such as a new car or a new house?

Only you can determine the priorities you want to follow in setting your financial goals and developing the strategies to reach them. However, no matter what your goals and strategies, you can avoid unpleasant and distracting surprises if you know at the outset how much you need for your personal financial affairs.

KEEPING RECORDS

You probably keep much of this information on hand to file your income taxes, but you should make sure that your financial records are clearly organized and accessible. As an entrepreneur, especially in the initial stages of your business, disorganization will only distract you from more pressing concerns. Besides, you're now responsible for paying yourself and making sure that you can meet your financial obligations. The more clearly you understand those obligations, the more easily you can get on with your business. And, if something happens to you, the people who depend on you will have an easier time coping if they know that their personal finances are in order.

Your records should include:

- Household income and expense records,
- Unpaid bills, indicating dates when they have to be paid,
- Photocopies of personal documents including credit cards, passports, birth and marriage certificates, mortgage and loan documents, automobile loan agreements, and so on. Anyone who has ever lost these documents knows how difficult it can be to replace them without copies.
- Insurance policies,

- Receipts for equipment and luxuries such as computers, jewellery, art, antiques, and stereos,
- Records of bank accounts, stocks, bonds, GICs, and so on,
- Addresses and phone numbers of advisers such as your accountant, lawyer, insurance agent, and banker.

HOLD ON TO YOUR CASH AS LONG AS YOU CAN

The better you maintain cash flow in your personal life, the better you can concentrate on your business. Most fixed expenses have to be paid at regular intervals. You should indicate on a calendar the dates when these bills have to be paid. As a good cash manager, you should pay them as late as possible, but on time. Why give someone else the use of your money before you have to?

CASH FLOW

You know exactly when you have to meet your financial obligations to other people, including the phone company, the mortgage company, the credit card company, and Revenue Canada. Other people are less predictable when it comes to paying you. As a result, you may not feel confident that you'll have cash on hand to meet your regular expenses.

To alleviate your discomfort, you might do one of two things. First, you can calculate your receivables and determine how much money your business can expect to receive over the next month, two months, and three months. Will it cover your salary? How reliable are the customers who owe you money?

Or, you can obtain a personal line of credit sufficient to cover expenses for a period of several months. You can then meet your personal financial obligations without anxiety. You can cover the cost of servicing your line of credit by increasing the salary that you receive from your company, coordinating your pricing to accommodate your personal obligations, or arranging your business finances to reflect the uncertainty of your personal situation.

KEEPING A CLEAN CREDIT RECORD

Before they approve a loan or a line of credit, banks evaluate an applicant's business and personal credit history, through electronic links to one of Canada's two national credit bureaus. All Canadians who have borrowed money have established a credit history that reflects their repayment habits, current address, and employer's name. This information is gathered from public records and lenders such as financial institutions, department stores, and oil companies. Your credit history includes information on former loans, mortgages, and outstanding credit card balances. It indicates the nature of the loan, how quickly you repaid it, whether a lender has ever turned over a loan to a collection agency, and whether you've ever gone bankrupt. Unfavourable information such as a bankruptcy is kept on file for about seven years. Multiple bankruptcies are recorded permanently.

Your individual credit rating consists of two elements, indicated by a combination of letters and numbers.

Letters indicate the type of loan.

- "R" stands for revolving credit such as a credit card, which enables a borrower to make purchases up to a specified limit and repay the balance over time.
- "I" stands for installment credit such as a mortgage or car loan, with a defined term and regular payments.
- "O" stands for open credit, such as an American Express card, on which the borrower pays the balance in full each month.

Numbers indicate the borrower's promptness in repaying debts.

- Zero represents a new, unused account.
- One indicates that the borrower pays within a specified payment schedule, usually within 30 days.
- Nine identifies a bad debt that has been written off by the lender.

If you plan to apply for a loan, your credit history will play a critical role in the process, so you should make sure that yours is accurate. Errors can occur when you move, obtain a new credit card, or get married or divorced. There's also a good chance that someone else has the same name as yours, without necessarily sharing your good judgment and prudent spending habits. If you find an error, the credit bureau must correct it and notify lenders of any changes. If you and the lender disagree about your credit rating, a note is attached to your history explaining the difference of opinion.

You can obtain your own credit history by contacting the bureaus directly. Usually you'll need photocopies of two pieces of identification, along with proof of your current address, taken from a utility bill or credit card invoice. Mail this information to: Equifax Canada Inc., Box 190, Station Jean-Talon, Montreal, Quebec H1S 2Z2 (1-800-465-7166) or Trans Union of Canada, Consumer Relations Centre, P.O. Box 338-LCD1, Hamilton, Ontario L8L 7W2 (416-291-7032). They will mail the appropriate information to you in about two weeks.

your
personal
financial plan

Money may not bring happiness. You'll have to take care of that yourself. But it brings a lot of other things that contribute to our well-being and prosperity, from housing, food, and clothing to education and vacations. The better you plan your finances, the better you can determine where you want to spend your money. By planning your personal and business finances, you can make better decisions and take greater control of your personal and business life.

3

A good plan doesn't answer questions; it allows you to choose the appropriate answers for your particular circumstances. If you ask yourself what you want your money to contribute to your life, the answer you choose at the age of 25 will likely differ from the one you choose at 40 or 65. This doesn't mean you were wrong at one age and right at another; it just means that your circumstances evolve along with your needs.

The better you understand your financial situation at any particular point in your development, the better decisions you can make about your personal and business life. You may not lose everything if you don't plan, but you'll gain far more from your resources if you do.

LIFESTYLE VERSUS GROWTH

Your personal goals and objectives play a critical role in determining the kind of business you want to build. Your personal financial plan, based on your aspirations, attributes, and circumstances, will exert a major influence on your business goals and your strategy for reaching them.

As Amar Bhide points out, "An entrepreneur's personal and business goals are inextricably linked. Financially, some entrepreneurs are looking for quick profits, some want to generate a satisfactory cash flow, and others seek capital gains from building and selling a company. Some entrepreneurs who want to build sustainable institutions do not consider personal financial returns a high priority. They may refuse acquisition proposals regardless of the price or sell equity cheaply to employees to secure their loyalty to the institution."

Your lifestyle, family circumstances, aspirations, and personality will determine the amount of money you need to generate from your business for your own use. They'll also determine the extent to which you're willing to sacrifice your current income for the sake of the future growth of your business.

By defining your characteristics and building a complementary financial plan, you can then determine how you want to proceed with your business.

In the meantime, you can also keep to a minimum the disruptive pressures that your business exerts on your family life. Entrepreneurs have a far better chance of success if their families understand and support their business aspirations.

FAMILY FORTUNES

A personal financial plan must accommodate your family's circumstances as well as your own. To this end, you have to answer a few questions before you proceed with your planning. Who manages the money in your family, for example? Your husband? Your wife? Is it a family affair? Or do you just play it by ear?

Usually one spouse takes charge of the money. And when that person unexpectedly leaves or dies, the other has to figure out where the money is, what investments they own, and how much insurance they have. This can cause hardships even before a crisis occurs.

In fact, everyone should be involved in the family fortune, even the kids. That way, in the event of a death or breakup, it will be much easier for the others to pick up the pieces.

MONEY ISSUES

One of the biggest causes of marital tension is ambiguity over each member's financial responsibilities. Blithely assuming that "what's yours is mine, and what's mine is yours" is a prescription for disaster. You must decide in advance how you'll divide the money. There are three choices:

1. Ideally the larger salary pays for the basic expenses—things like the rent or mortgage, electric bill, food, insurance, and so on. The smaller salary pays for investments, holidays, and unexpected purchases. However, in the real world, it usually takes both salaries just to cover the basics, let alone investments. Still, you should try to set aside some money for investment purposes, regardless of where the money comes from.

2. The second scenario involves opening a joint daily-interest savings account. Both spouses deposit all their money into this account. They pay all the bills from this account. They use what's left over for investments, holidays, and unexpected purchases. In addition, both spouses receive a monthly allowance to spend as they please. But if one spouse contributes significantly more than the other to the joint account, arguments can develop.

3. The third scenario involves running the family finances like a business. Both spouses decide how much money they need each month to cover their day-to-day expenses plus investments and special purchases. Then each spouse contributes a certain percentage of his or her salary to cover these expenses. They can each do as they please with the remainder of their money. The benefit of this plan is that you don't have to ask anyone's permission to spend the remainder of your money.

REVISING YOUR PLAN

Your personal circumstances will change as time passes, just as your business will change as it evolves. In your personal life, the financial concerns you face in your twenties will differ substantially from the concerns you have to deal with at retirement. In both your business and your personal life, it makes sense to review your goals and your financial plan periodically.

According to some commentators, people go through four stages in their financial life cycles.

1. The early earnings period (early 20s to mid-30s): At this stage, financial concerns are generally basic and immediate: Establishing a credit record, negotiating a mortgage, beginning to save for children's education, and eventually building a modest savings/investment portfolio.

2. The mid-earnings period (early 30s to mid-40s): By this age, you feel more financially secure and the long-term growth of your savings/investment portfolio will become a greater priority.

3. Pre-retirement: Many people begin to prepare for retirement between the ages of 45 and 60, depending on their personal financial situation. Children may be leaving the nest, although care for aging parents may be a personal and financial concern.

4. Retirement: Once you've reached retirement, you'll likely focus your concerns on generating enough money to live on, with a predictable cash flow fed by well-protected assets. If you haven't done this already, you'll also start planning your estate and the transfer of assets to your children.

At each of these stages you'll have different personal and financial objectives. You'll also develop different financial strategies for attaining them.

The following pages provide some guidelines, reminders, and background about the issues you'll have to consider in developing a personal financial plan.

ELEMENTS OF THE PLAN

1. YOUR HEALTH AND YOUR HOME

Good health is a prerequisite for starting a business. The pressures and challenges of building a business will take their toll on even the the most robust individual. Anxiety, apprehension, and tension, aggravated by long hours, are part of the job as an entrepreneur, and they will only aggravate an illness or chronic infirmity.

They can also contribute to illness at a later date, so it makes sense to maintain a healthy regimen despite the restrictions of your work. Eat well, stay fit, try to get as much sleep as you can—all the things your parents told you make sense, now more than ever.

As an entrepreneur, you can no longer resort to your employer's group insurance plans to cover the cost of treatment or disability for you or your family. You may have arranged similar plans to cover employees and your-self within your own operation, but one way or the other, you now pay for what your employer used to provide in the form of insurance. Make sure you get the coverage you need, and that you don't jeopardize your family's health care by cutting costs in your insurance planning.

MAXIMIZE YOUR MEDICAL EXPENSE CREDIT

For tax purposes, the lower-income spouse should claim all
medical costs, as long as he or she has taxable income.

2. LIFE INSURANCE: WHO NEEDS IT?

Life insurance protects the value of your estate for your financial depen-dents in the event of your death. Anyone who has financial dependents should make sure he or she has sufficient life insurance.

SINGLE? WHY BUY LIFE INSURANCE?

If you're single, with no dependents, you don't need life insurance unless you want to leave a fortune to your goldfish.
Instead, you should invest your money so you can eventually
become self-insured.

If you have no children and both spouses work, you probably don't need life insurance. If you have children, then you should consider low-cost term insurance until the children can support themselves. If your spouse doesn't earn an income or works only part-time, but is responsible for caring for the children, then life insurance is necessary to cover unex-pected child-care expenses.

If your children have grown up and left home, your mortgage is all paid off, and most of your debts paid down, then you probably need little, if any, life insurance.

HOW MUCH DO YOU NEED?

To determine your life insurance needs, do some simple calculations.

1. Determine how much family income you need each year to maintain your current lifestyle.

2. Figure out how much each spouse contributes to the family income, in money or services.

3. Multiply each spouse's contribution by ten. The ten represents a 10% minimum annual return from your investments.

For instance, if your family requires $50,000 a year to maintain its current lifestyle, then multiply $50,000 by 10 to get $500,000.

Your family needs $500,000 worth of life insurance. If the money were invested at 10%, the family could maintain its current lifestyle.

There are three insurance options: Whole life, universal, and term life insurance.

WHOLE LIFE INSURANCE

Although over 80% of insured Canadians have either whole-life or universal life insurance policies, whole-life policies are financially unsound choices. Whole-life is simply life insurance with a savings plan attached to it. The savings are called the cash value of the plan.

For example: The typical $100,000 whole-life policy for a 35-year-old will probably cost about $1,300 a year. In the first year, the agent's commission is about $900. The average annual interest paid to your savings plan, or the plan's cash value, is about 2%.

After paying a $1,300 yearly premium for 20 years, you'll have paid $26,000 in premiums. Even if you earn 3% annually, your plan will have a cash value of about $35,000. That's not much to show for 20 years of saving.

In the meantime, since your own money is accumulating in the plan, the insurance company will let you borrow it—at an interest rate of 5% to

8%. In other words, you get to pay interest to borrow your own money. The amount that you don't pay back will be subtracted from the death benefit that your beneficiaries receive.

PARTICIPATE OR NOT

If you receive dividend payments from your life insurance policy, you have a participating policy. If you don't receive any dividend payments, you have a non-participating policy.

In most cases, the dividends that you receive are not returned profits but rather your own money that you overpaid in premiums in the first place. Revenue Canada does not treat as special these dividends, so you have to pay taxes on them just as you would pay taxes on interest income.

UNIVERSAL LIFE INSURANCE

This is a life insurance policy with an unimpressive investment vehicle attached. The investment vehicle usually pays a fixed rate of interest, and sometimes takes the form of a stock mutual fund.

Many policies promise to pay you 8% to 10% on your investment, but that figure will be calculated on what remains of your money after everything else is deducted. The typical $100,000 universal life insurance policy costs about $2,000 a year in premiums. During the first year, about $600—about 30% of your investment—will cover fees and commissions. Another $300 will pay for the actual life insurance coverage. That leaves about $1,100 of your original policy, which is the actual amount that earns the promised 8% to 10% return in the first year.

As the years pass, less and less of your premium will go toward your investment plan, so your return will actually diminish over time. Finally, if you decide to cancel, you may have to pay a surrender charge.

TERM LIFE INSURANCE

Intelligent investors buy term life insurance and invest the difference themselves. A term life insurance policy has no savings or investment vehicle attached to it. It's the lowest-priced life insurance available.

Term insurance is a temporary form of insurance that provides coverage when you need it, and the option to cancel when you no longer need it. As with car or house insurance, you don't collect unless something happens. In this case, you have to die.

There are three types of term policies: Yearly renewable term, decreasing term, and level premium term.

Yearly Renewable Term

This is just what it says: a life insurance policy for just one year, at the end of which you either renew for another year or cancel. Although the premiums will increase each year as you age, this plan remains the cheapest type of term insurance.

Your renewal can be guaranteed each year to age 90, providing you pay your premiums on time.

If you have only a short-term need for life insurance, then yearly renewable term is your best bet.

Decreasing Term Insurance

Your yearly premiums stay the same, but the amount of life insurance coverage decreases each year. Eventually your yearly premiums become very overpriced. This type of term insurance is not a good deal.

Level Premium Term Insurance

If you have long-term life insurance needs, this is your best choice. You select the length of coverage you want—10, 15, or 20-year term, even 100 years. Your yearly premiums and the amount of life insurance coverage remain the same for the length of the term.

MORTGAGE LIFE INSURANCE

Mortgage life insurance will pay off the outstanding amount of your mortgage if you die. It costs about $30 to $50 a month per $100,000 of mortgage principal. However, if you die 20 years from now, you'll have perhaps $15,000 left to pay on today's $100,000 mortgage. So your death triggers the payment of $15,000 to your survivors. That means you've paid $30 to $50 a month for 20 years, to provide your family with a measly $15,000 when you go.

If you die in the last year of your mortgage, when you've paid it down to $1,000, your family gets $1,000 back after all those years of sweat and toil.

AN ALTERNATIVE TO MORTGAGE LIFE INSURANCE

As an alternative, buy a $100,000 term life insurance policy. If you die in the 20th year of the policy, your family gets $100,000, no matter how much remains of your mortgage. If you've paid off everything but the last $15,000, your family can pay it off with the insurance money and still have $85,000 remaining.

3. ATTORNEY POWER

A power of attorney doesn't describe the weight-bearing capacity of a muscle-bound lawyer. A power of attorney actually ensures that your affairs will be well managed during periods when you may be incapacitated.

If you're mentally or physically incapable of administering your own affairs, the person to whom you've given power of attorney can take complete control of your financial affairs. He or she can sign cheques, allocate dividend payments to your bank accounts, and make other financial decisions on your behalf.

A lawyer—muscle-bound or otherwise—can handle the paperwork when you designate someone to hold power of attorney.

A LIVING WILL

It's not unusual for a loved one to require care to survive. But how much care is enough? Do you want to be kept alive by artificial means? Do you want to be resuscitated after you've stopped breathing? Do you want to be kept alive even though you're in a coma and unlikely ever to regain full consciousness?

With a living will, you can relieve your family of these agonizing decisions. A living will simply describes the level of care you want if you become terminally ill. Your lawyer can help you draft it.

4. SMART KIDS

If you want to save now for your children's future education, you can use a Registered Education Savings Plan (RESP). With a RESP, you can contribute up $1,500 a year, and no more than $31,500 over the life of the plan, for each of your children, grandchildren, great-grandchildren, and so on.

The amount you contribute to a RESP cannot be deducted from your taxable income. However, the income generated inside the plan can accumulate tax free for up to 25 years.

If the RESP's beneficiary decides not to go to school, you can transfer the funds to another beneficiary, who must be a full-time student attending a post-secondary institution.

If no beneficiary uses the RESP funds to attend a post-secondary institution, you can take back all the money that you contributed to the plan. But you lose all the tax-free compounding.

If you're not sure that your children will continue with their post-secondary education (and fewer than 50% do), you can make money on your investments elsewhere and still contribute to their expenses if your children change their minds.

You can open a mutual fund in your child's name, for example, using the child's monthly tax-credit cheque or your own money.

If you invest $1,000 each year into a good quality equity mutual fund, the 16% to 18% annual return your child will receive will turn that $1,000 annual contribution into $50,000 to $60,000 over a 15-year period. Over a 20-year period, it could easily turn into more than $100,000. That buys a lot of textbooks.

TAX BITES

If you invest the child's tax credit cheque, any money that the child earns should not be attributed back to the parents. If you give your child the money to invest, the rules are a little different.

For children under age 18, capital gains earned from money given to a child are not attributed back to the parents. Since most of a stock mutual fund's appreciation comes from capital gains, the majority of the gains will stay in the child's name and not be attributed back to you. However, interest and dividend income is attributed back to the contributing parent.

Income-splitting strategies also make a difference at tax time. Married and common-law couples can take advantage of a number of strategies that shift income from the higher-income spouse to the lower-income spouse. For tax purposes, this reduces the taxable income of the higher-income spouse, while the one with the lower income pays tax at a lower rate. For example, your spouse can provide you with a business service for which you can pay out of your income.

5. RETIREMENT PLANNING

You may plan never to retire. You like running a business so much that you intend to do it forever. Call this non-retirement planning if you like, but it still requires a plan. Besides, you might change your mind, and the more options you give yourself, the better the choice that you'll eventually make.

Canadians who reach the age of 65 without major health problems live, on average, for another 20 years. To maintain your standard of living, you'll need about 70% of your pre-retirement income.

Funding your retirement is your responsibility. As an entrepreneur, you'll have to construct your own personal and corporate pension plans. You should put your plan in place before you become preoccupied with other demands of your business.

REGISTERED RETIREMENT SAVINGS PLANS

Regardless of the quality of your company pension plan, you and your family will need Registered Retirement Savings Plans (RRSPs) to take full advantage of the opportunities to accumulate wealth tax free. In fact, if your children are fortunate enough start an RRSP when they're young, they'll never have to worry when they're old.

On money held in an RRSP, you pay no taxes. When you put money into an RRSP, you can deduct an equivalent amount from your total annual income when you're calculating your income tax for the year. That means you pay less tax, and your money grows tax free.

An RRSP is a critical component of your financial plan. Within an RRSP, you can move money around from GICs, for example, to mutual funds to stocks and bonds, without losing its tax-free status.

Outside an RRSP, your money may earn $100, and you'd pay, say, $25 in tax, leaving you with $75. Inside an RRSP, your money may make $100, and you'd pay no tax. So you still have $100 left to reinvest.

RRSP CONTRIBUTION LIMITS

You can contribute up to 18% of your earned income from the previous years, to a maximum of $13,500.

That limit applies to all your contributions to a registered pension fund, whether you make them yourself or through your company pension plan.

Your money grows tax free within the RRSP. You also get the benefit of a tax deduction. If you earn $40,000 a year, for example, your marginal tax rate will be about 42%. If you contribute $5,000 to an RRSP, you'll save $2,100 in taxes. If you hadn't invested $5,000 in an RRSP, you'd pay that tax—$2,100—to the government.

RRSP IN ACTION

If you invest that $5,000 in a good mutual fund, you should be able to earn 15% to 18% a year, on average. At 15% a year, that $5,000 will become $20,250 in just 10 years.

THE DETAILS ABOUT RRSPS

You don't have to take your tax deduction in the same year as you make your contribution. You can claim it in any future year. If your income goes up in a couple of years, as it likely will if your business grows, you'll have to pay tax at a higher rate. The more you make, the more the government takes.

If you're taxed at a higher rate, then your contribution is worth more in terms of the money you'll save in taxes.

Nor do you have to make your maximum contribution this year. You can add the amount remaining of this year's eligible contribution to your contribution next year, or the year after that, for up to seven years.

For example, say your 1997 maximum RRSP contribution was $5,700 and you contributed only $3,700. You're still eligible to contribute $2,000, and you can make this contribution any time over the next seven years, in addition to your maximum annual contribution for the year.

Because they have to pay tax on the money when they remove it from an RRSP, many people wonder why they should bother investing in an RRSP at all. But even after you pay the tax when you remove your money from an RRSP, you still end up with substantially more than you'd have if you'd invested it outside an RRSP.

Here's an example: Ms. A invests $5,000 inside an RRSP. Mr. B invests $5,000 outside an RRSP. Each pays tax at a rate of 52% and earns 12% a year on the invested money.

After 20 years, Ms. A has more than $70,000. Mr. B has less than $34,000.

ELIGIBLE RRSP INVESTMENTS

You can keep almost any type of investment in your RRSP, from the soup of equities to the nuts of bonds. In general, the following investments qualify:

1. GICs and term deposits
2. Money deposited in Canadian funds in a bank, trust company, or credit union
3. Mutual funds registered with Revenue Canada
4. Certain bonds (including CSBs), debentures, and similar obligations guaranteed by the Government of Canada, a province, a municipality, or a Crown corporation
5. Shares, rights, warrants, and call options listed on stock exchanges in Montreal, Toronto, Winnipeg, Alberta, or Vancouver
6. Shares of unlisted Canadian public corporations
7. Shares listed on prescribed foreign stock exchanges, including Paris, London, New York, Mexican, National, Pacific Coast, Boston, Philadelphia-Baltimore, Chicago Board of Trade, Washington, Cincinnati, Pittsburgh, Detroit, Salt Lake, Mid West, Spokane, The American Exchange, and the NASDAQ (National Association of Securities Dealers Automated Quotation system)
8. A bond, debenture, note, or similar obligation issued by a public corporation

9. A mortgage secured by real property located in Canada, as long as certain conditions are met
10. Mortgage-backed securities
11. Qualifying retirement annuities
12. Shares of small business corporations, subject to stringent requirements

For entrepreneurs, there are opportunitites to make RRSP investments in your own company, under certain circumstances. A tax adviser can help you with the details. However, you should exercise caution if you pursue this option. Just as you shouldn't put all your financial eggs in one basket, you should certainly avoid putting your entire retirement nest egg in a single investment.

BOOK VALUE, MARKET VALUE, AND FOREIGN CONTENT

The book value of your RRSP is simply the amount of money that you've contributed to the plan. Its market value is the amount that your RRSP investments would fetch if you sold them all today.

If you contribute $1,000 to your RRSP, buying 100 shares of a mutual fund trading at $10 per share, your RRSP's book value will be $1,000. If the share price rises to $15, your RRSP's market value will increase to $1,500. But its book value remains at $1,000.

This becomes an important consideration if you invest in foreign equities. Under current regulations, you can invest up to 20% of your RRSP's book value outside of Canada. The foreign content of your RRSP can include mutual funds that invest primarily outside of Canada or individual stocks of companies that have incorporated outside of Canada. Almost all shares traded on the New York, American, or NASDAQ Stock Exchanges are considered to be foreign content.

If a foreign mutual fund rises substantially in value, it won't throw your RRSP's foreign-content ratio out of whack. However, dividends from stocks in your RRSP that are automatically reinvested can add to the RRSP's book value. If your RRSP's foreign content exceeds the limit, the government will charge you 1% of the excess per month.

The financial institution that holds your RRSP will calculate the percentage of foreign exposure and let you know if you exceed the limit.

INVESTMENT TIP

We should all try to maximize the foreign content in our RRSPs. Here's why: All the money that's invested in Canada adds up to only 3% of all the money in the world. That means 97% of the action goes on somewhere else.

Currency rates are another reason to invest outside Canada. In 1991, the Canadian dollar was worth US89¢. Three years later, it was worth US72¢. If you held a U.S. investment, and all it did was break even, you would have made money, because your U.S. dollars would be worth more than they were when you made the investment.

SELF-DIRECTED RRSPS

With a self-directed RRSP, you can include different investments within the same plan. These might include a Canada Trust GIC, a Royal Bank term deposit, various stocks, bonds, mutual funds, mortgage-backed securities, strip-coupon bonds, and CSBs.

Within a self-directed plan, you can change your investment mix at any time. If one financial institution offers a better deal than the others, you can switch. And you no longer have to worry about deposit insurance, because you can put $60,000 in CIBC GICs, $60,000 in TD Bank term deposits, and so on.

Most financial institutions handle self-administered RRSPs and charge an administration fee of about $100 to $150 for the service. You can deduct these administration fees from your taxable income. However, you can't deduct brokerage fees charged for the purchase or sale of securities within an RRSP.

The flexibility you get from a self-directed RRSP is usually worth the fee.

SPOUSAL RRSPS

If you're legally married, you can contribute a portion or all of your allowable contribution to your spouse's RRSP.

If your spouse earns less than you do and pays tax at a lower rate, then you both save on income tax. First, you claim the tax deduction, even though you contribute to your spouse's RRSP. Then, when your spouse withdraws the money from the spousal plan, your spouse reports the income and pays the taxes, presumably at a lower rate.

You have to leave the money in the plan for two years or more. Otherwise, the contributing spouse gets taxed.

If your spouse has no earned income, you can still contribute on your spouse's behalf to an RRSP. You can contribute even if your spouse has already made the maximum contribution to an RRSP. It is your contribution that matters.

INCLUDE YOUR SPOUSE

A spousal RRSP also allows the older spouse to transfer funds to the younger spouse's plan, allowing funds to appreciate, tax free, for a longer period. You can contribute to your spouse's RRSP even if you're over age 69—the maximum age for contributing to an RRSP—providing you still have earned income and your spouse is not over the age of 69.

HOME BUYER'S PLAN

Introduced in the 1992 federal budget, the Home Buyer's Plan allows individuals to withdraw funds tax free from their RRSPs and use the money to purchase a home from someone else. Then they have to pay the money back to their RRSP. The home can take the form of a house, mobile home, apartment, condominium, or co-operative.

You can withdraw up to $20,000 tax free. That means a couple can withdraw up to $40,000. You have to pay the money back over 15 equal annual installments. The payments are not tax deductible. If you miss a payment or make only a partial payment, then your taxable income will increase by the amount of the shortfall.

If you borrow $15,000 from your RRSP, for example, then you'll have to repay it in annual installments of $1,000 apiece over the next 15 years. If you pay only $600 in a particular year, you'll have to pay tax on the remaining $400 that you failed to repay.

The first installment must be made by the end of the second year following the year of the withdrawal. If you removed the money in

1996, the first installment payment would not be due until the end of 1998.

Before you can remove the money from your RRSP, you must have a written agreement to acquire a qualifying home that will be used as your primary residence within one year of purchase. The home must be located in Canada, and it must be your main year-round residence.

It doesn't matter whether the home is new, used, or under construction. Nor does it matter whether this is the first home you've ever bought. However, you cannot use the plan to pay for a home that you've already purchased.

Participants in the plan can make RRSP contributions in the same year in which they make the withdrawal. But you have to make the contribution at least 91 days before you withdraw the money.

GOOD POINTS AND BAD

Once you remove money from your RRSP to buy a home, it's a lot harder than you think to recover the lost earnings of your tax-sheltered funds. Say, for example, at age 31, you withdraw $10,000 from your RRSP and use it as a down payment on a house. Then you pay back the money in 15 annual installments. At age 71, you'll have about $85,000 in your RRSP, assuming a 7% annual return.

If you'd left the money in your RRSP to compound tax free, assuming that same 7% yield, you'd have about $150,000 in the plan at age 71.

THE BEST INVESTMENTS

Your goal in your RRSP should be maximum yield through long-term growth. You can obtain it from a diversified portfolio of mutual funds.

You don't have to keep all of it in mutual funds. But you should invest at least some of it there. Even if they return just 1% more than your other investments, they can still make a huge difference down the road.

A solid conservative RRSP portfolio might consist of Canadian and foreign equity funds, income and bond funds, some GICs, CSBs, money market funds, and gold. The equity fund provides the maximum long-term growth. The income and bond funds provide the steady stream of income, year after year. The cash component of the portfolio is the slush fund, providing both safety and available capital to scoop up bargains as prices fall in other areas. The gold fund provides potential for growth while maintaining purchasing power.

THE HIGH COST OF RETIREMENT

Retirement is a lot more expensive than you might anticipate. If you have $100,000 earning 4% in the bank, for example, and you want to remove $15,000 a year to cover your living expenses, it will take only seven years to run out of money. At 10%, you could remove $15,000 for 10 years before your $100,000 ran out.

BORROWING AND OTHER TIPS AND CALCULATIONS

If you don't have enough cash on hand to maximize your RRSP contribution, you should consider borrowing the money. Interest on money borrowed for RRSPs is not deductible. But it can still be worth borrowing, as long as you can pay back the loan within a year. The longer it takes to pay back the money, the less benefit you'll receive.

Most financial institutions will lend you the money at the prime interest rate, providing you purchase your RRSP through that institution.

Let's say, for example, your maximum RRSP contribution is $8,000, and you have only $5,000 to invest.

If you borrow the other $3,000 from the bank and pay 7% interest on the loan, and you earn 7% on your RRSP investment, it really doesn't make much difference whether you borrowed to invest or not. You pay 7%; and you earn 7%. However, once you pay off the loan, your investment continues to compound tax free.

The clincher, though, is the tax rebate. If you're in the 42% marginal tax bracket, that $3,000 contribution will provide you with a rebate of $1,260. Now you're way ahead of the game. You can use that money to reinvest in your business or apply to personal expenses.

WHAT HAPPENS WHEN I'M 69

In the year you turn 69, you have to decide if you want to

1. Roll your plan into a Registered Retirement Income Fund (RRIF) and/or;
2. Liquidate your RRSP assets and buy one or more annuities with the proceeds and/or;
3. Cash in your RRSP.

A RRIF or annuity allows you to continue sheltering your assets accumulated within the RRSP. But an annuity requires more planning, since you should monitor interest rates for several years before you make your purchase.

If you cash in your RRSP, you pay tax on the full value, which will likely push you into a higher tax bracket. You also lose the protection of a tax shelter, in which some of your financial assets can accumulate tax free.

If you neglect to convert your RRSP to an annuity or a RRIF, the government will tax the full value of your assets contained within the plan.

REGISTERED RETIREMENT INCOME FUNDS

A RRIF is a tax-sheltered plan just like an RRSP, except that assets in an RRSP accumulate as you contibute to your plan, while assets in a RRIF eventually diminish as you withdraw money from your plan. You can create the same kind of diversified investment portfolio, tailored to your needs and your risk level, as you held in your RRSP. A RRIF may also be self-directed.

With a RRIF, you are legally obligated to withdraw a minimum amount per year. Within this guideline, you choose the withdrawal amounts and the withdrawal schedule, depending on your needs and lifestyle. You can withdraw assets in cash or in its equivalent value in the form of mutual fund units or other investments. Although you still have to pay tax on the withdrawal, you can preserve your asset instead of cashing it in.

RRIF OPTIONS

Starting the year after you open your RRIF, you have to withdraw at least the legally required minimum from your fund every year. You may also choose to withdraw more than the minimum in fixed amounts each year or to withdraw an amount that increases by a percentage each year.

If you choose one of these options, you'll deplete your RRIF much more quickly than if you choose to withdraw the minimum payment.

REGISTERED PENSION PLANS AND DEFERRED PROFIT SHARING PLANS

Depending on the province where you live, you have to convert your Registered Pension Plan (RPP) or Deferred Profit Sharing Plan (DPSP) into a retirement income plan when you reach a specific age. Your options include:

- A locked-in RRSP,
- A Life Income Fund (LIF), and
- A Life Income Retirement Account.

With a locked-in RRSP, you can't withdraw the funds before retirement without paying a tax penalty. You may also have to convert the plan to a LIF or a LIRA when you reach 69. A LIF is just like a RRIF, except that there is a maximum as well as a minimum annual withdrawal. A LIRA gives you a number of years in which you can monitor interest rates so you can purchase your annuity when rates are favourable. In the interim, you manage your locked-in funds as you would a RRIF. You have to convert your LIRA to an annuity by a specific age.

ANNUITIES

Annuities guarantee a predetermined level of retirement income while maintaining the tax-sheltered status of your RRSP funds. Less flexible than RRIFs, annuities are locked-in, interest-bearing investments that pay you income for life or until you reach age 90. Couples can purchase a joint annuity, and payments continue until the death of the surviving spouse.

You may have as many annuities as you want, and you can hold a combination of RRIFs and annuities.

Annuities depend on interest to maintain the purchasing power of your retirement savings, so you should shop carefully for the right annuity and the right interest rate. If interest rates are low when you retire, consider holding your funds in a RRIF until rates recover.

There are basically three types of annuities: term certain, single life, and joint and last survivor.

Term Certain Annuities

You receive payments for a fixed term. If you die before the term is up, your estate receives the payments.

Single Life Annuities

This is the simplest type of annuity. You receive monthly payments for as long as you live.

Joint and Last Survivor Life Annuities

Both you and your spouse continue to receive payments as long as either of you remains alive. The monthly payments are lower than they would be from a single life.

You can also choose an index, or escalating rate, annuity. This gives you monthly payments that never decrease, but may increase based on an interest-rate indicator. Your monthly payments will be lower than those of a straight life annuity during the early years, but the payments will eventually increase if and when interest rates rise.

LOOK BEFORE YOU LEAP

With most annuities, you're locked in for life at the prevailing interest rate when you sign the contract. If you buy one when interest rates are low, you'll feel the crunch when inflation and interest rates start rising.

For example, say your fixed yearly payment is $10,000, and inflation rises to 5% a year. In 20 years, you'll need over $25,000 to maintain the purchasing power of today's $10,000. But since your payments are fixed, your purchasing power will fall.

To address this problem, some insurance companies sell cashable or retractable annuities. You can cash these annuities early, and then renegotiate your annuity once interest rates rise.

Better still, forget about an annuity and go for a RRIF.

YOUR MINIMUM RRIF WITHDRAWAL

If you're under 69, take the number 90, subtract your age, and divide the amount of the RRIF by the resulting number.

For instance: You're 65 years old. You've got $100,000 in your RRIF. To find out how much you have to withdraw per year, subtract 65 from 90, which leaves you with 25. Now divide $100,000 by 25: That comes to $4,000. That means you have to withdraw $4,000 in the first year of your RRIF.

In each following year, you use the same calculation (90 minus your age, divided into the total market value of the RRIF).

When you reach age 69, you have to use a different calculation to determine the minimum withdrawal. Since RRIF payments are now received for life, a specific factor is used in calculating the minimum withdrawal.

RRIFs offer the best opportunity for deferring your taxes for the longest possible time.

LIVE LONG AND PROSPER

Canadians live longer than ever these days. In fact, about 25% of men and 39% of woman who reach age 69 will live past 90. And each of them will need money to live.

RETIREMENT FUNDS AND ESTATE PLANNING

You should designate your spouse or a financially dependent child as the beneficiary of your RRSP or RRIF. Then, if you die, your spouse can put the money tax free into his or her RRSP or RRIF.

You may also designate your spouse as a successor annuitant. In the event of your death, your spouse will receive RRIF payments just as you did, while continuing to manage the RRIF and make investment decisions. The assets within the plan remain tax sheltered.

If there's no surviving spouse and the RRSP/RRIF funds are left to a financially dependent child or grandchild, the funds will be taxed at the child's marginal tax rate or used to purchase an annuity until the child turns 18.

If there's no surviving spouse and no children under age 18, the money goes to your estate and is reported as income on your final tax return.

Annuities work slightly differently. A fixed-term annuity makes payments to you or a designated beneficiary until the end of the term. If the beneficiary dies before the end of the term, the value of the annuity is paid to the estate—unless you've made other arrangements.

A life annuity ceases to make payments on the death of the annuitant.

A joint life annuity continues to make payments to a surviving spouse until the spouse dies. There are no residual payments to the estate.

FIGHT OR FLIGHT

Fed up with Canadian winters? You can spend up to six months out of the country and maintain your resident status for the purpose of taxes, health insurance, and other benefits. If you stay away longer, you may have to prove your resident status by maintaining a principal residence, bank accounts, or other interests in Canada.

When you cease to be a Canadian resident, payments from Canadian sources—your RRIF, annuity payments, and income from investments and profit-sharing plans—are subject to a withholding tax. As a foreign resident, you are also subject to applicable foreign property taxes, income taxes, and succession duties—whether or not you remain a Canadian citizen.

6. OTHER CONSIDERATIONS

There are other considerations to address in your plan, too.

1. Your choice of a retirement home: This will have a significant effect on your financial plan. The easiest choice is to remain in the family home. But you may not want to maintain a large home and garden, especially if you plan to travel.

2. Home equity: If you want money for retirement, you can take advantage of the equity in your home without selling it outright, using a reverse mortgage or a secured line of credit. The older you are, the more money a lender will advance on a reverse mortgage. You can obtain a line of credit, secured by a mortgage, for an amount equivalent to 75% of the value of your home.

3. Divorce: The financial impact of divorce can be devastating, especially if it occurs just before you retire. Depending on the province, you may have to split the value

of your matrimonial home, your retirement investments, Canada Pension Plan, company pension plan benefits, and the assets of your own business. If you haven't married yet, you should consider a prenuptial agreement to protect your assets in the event of marriage breakdown. If you want to provide for children from a previous marriage, you should consult an estate planner.

7. ESTATE PLANNING

Estate planning ensures your assets are distributed according to your wishes, in a timely, tax-efficient way. With a little planning, you can preserve assets for your family, reduce taxes, and accommodate beneficiaries who have special needs. There are several elements to a sound estate plan.

THE WILL

A will gives you another chance to eliminate uncertainty from your financial life. You may not know exactly when you'll die, but you can determine exactly where your money goes when you do. And you can direct as much as possible to your family and away from the taxman.

There are two types of will: outright disposition and trust.

An outright disposition will names the beneficiaries who will receive your assets. The disposition of the assets usually occurs as soon as possible after your death.

A trust will places the assets inside a trust for the beneficiary. The trust contains two basic parts. The capital portion comprises the assets that are held inside the trust until the trust is dissolved. The income portion comprises the assets that will provide a regular income to the beneficiary.

When the trust is dissolved, the ultimate beneficiary receives all the assets. Trust wills are frequently left for children who, upon reaching a certain age, receive all the assets within the trust to spend as they please.

Without a will naming an executor, the court will designate an executor for you. And the government-appointed executor may or may not be the best person to do the job. As a result, your assets may not be distributed to your family and friends as you had planned. You can name one or more people as executors. The person (or people) you select should be honest, intelligent, and preferably younger than you.

CONTENTS OF A WILL

Here are the content of a basic will:

1. Your name, address, and occupation;

2. An explanation of how you want your assets to be distributed;

3. Your signature and the date on which you signed the will;

4. A note stating that you are revoking all of your previous wills;

5. The name of the person (or persons) whom you would like to act as executor(s) of the estate. You should also select a contingency person, just in case the first person(s) selected can't do the job.

6. Any special requests, such as leaving money to your favourite charity or donating your eyes to science.

7. A contingency clause to cover the distribution of your assets in the event that the primary beneficiary dies at the same time as you do.

8. The signatures of two witnesses (who are not beneficiaries) and their initials on each page of, and any changes made to, the will.

THE EXECUTOR

The executor makes sure that the provisions of your will are carried out. For example, the executor has to prove to the courts that the will is valid. This is known as probating the will. The executor is also responsible for

- Burying or disposing of your remains;
- Collecting any money owed to the estate;
- Paying all the debts owed by the estate (including income and estate taxes);
- Providing a list of the deceased's assets;
- Distributing the assets to the beneficiaries in accordance with the will.

The standard fee for the administrative services of the executor is approximately 4% of the value of the estate, providing that the assets are quickly distributable. However, if the assets are held inside a trust, then the trustee receives a care-and-management fee of approximately 0.25% each year based on the average market value of the estate. In addition, the trustee is usually allowed 5% per year of any income earned inside the trust.

These fees can sometimes be substantial; so, depending on the value of your estate, it makes sense to select someone whom you'd like to receive the money.

Most banks have trust departments that will act as executor for your estate, and many people choose to go this route. However, if your will is not complex, then you should consider a close friend or relative to act as executor.

If the executor is already familiar with your assets and beneficiaries, then so much the better. What you want to avoid is an executor with a conflict of interest.

Providing your children are over age 18, you should seriously consider giving them a role in the process. Not only will it be good experience for them in handling the assets, it will also save administrative fees.

One of the most popular choices for an executor is your lawyer. However, it is important to note that while lawyers may have superior knowledge of the administrative processes involved, they have little if any professional training when it comes to investing the funds.

On the other side of the coin, your accountant has professional training in taxes and estate planning, but lacks the administrative know-how of a lawyer.

If your will requires trusts to be set up and administered, then you should consider a trust company to act as trustee.

THE TRUSTEE

The trustee is responsible for administering a trust as long as it remains in force. Trust companies are qualified to administer and invest the funds in a competent manner. On the other hand, they are notoriously conservative money managers. In addition, beneficiaries often feel uncomfortable with the impersonal service that they receive from a trust company.

CHANGING YOUR WILL

Over time your circumstances change. You may get married, divorced, or have children, in which case you have to assign new beneficiaries. Just as it's important to revise your personal and business financial plan, it's prudent to review your will on a regular basis, and at least every five years.

If you plan to get married, you should note that, in most cases, marriage automatically revokes any previous wills made by the two partners.

But separation or divorce does not revoke a will unless a clause in the will specifically says that it should.

Also, death-tax provisions may change, which could affect the distribution of your assets.

If you decide to revise your will, you do not have to consult with any of the previously named beneficiaries.

OTHER TIPS ON WILLS

Here are some other tips about wills.

1. The best place to keep your will is with your lawyer. That way, in the event of your death, it can be easily retrieved. You should also keep an unsigned copy of the will in your files at home.

2. A husband and wife should have separate wills. Even if one partner doesn't have a career or very many assets in his or her own name, the person should still have a will. If the husband alone has a will, then his wife will receive all his assets upon his death. If she passes away before she has time to make a will, the government will decide what to do with the assets.

3. Outside Quebec, a new marriage invalidates your will, while a divorce doesn't. In some provinces, divorce may nullify a bequest to a former spouse.

4. If you have a will, it becomes effective as soon as you die. This can be a big advantage to your heirs, who otherwise wouldn't receive any assets for a long period. If you don't have a will, all the assets will be temporarily tied up, for months or even for years. Meanwhile, bills need to be paid and your estate managed. But there will be nobody to do it, because you didn't take the time to prepare your will.

5. A legal guardian looks after your children in the event that you and your spouse both die. Most people select the child's grandparents for the job. In fact, this isn't your best choice. That's because the grandparents are older. If they receive guardianship of your children and pass away soon after, the children suffer. A better choice is to find a younger couple you trust. But make sure that they're up to the job.

PLANNING FORMS

There are dozens of forms available to help you plan your personal finances. The following forms provide a general idea of the information that you need to compile to plan soundly. If you want more, check the appendices at the back of this book.

PERSONAL AND FAMILY INFORMATION

To apply for a loan or revise your will, you'll need a lot of information that you may not have at your fingertips. If you fill out this form completely, you won't have to scramble through the drawers looking for this information.

Form 3-1

Name _____ Birth date _____

Social Insurance Number _____

Spouse's name _____ Birth date _____

Social Insurance Number _____

Current address _____

Occupation _____

Business address _____

Phone _____

Spouse's occupation _____

Business address _____

Employer's name _____

Address _____

Phone _____

Job title _____

Children _____

Name _____ Birth date _____

Social insurance number _____

RETIREMENT PLANNING

As we've mentioned before, most Canadians do not plan adequately for their retirement. As a result, they either continue working, whether they like it or not, or live on a meagre income that doesn't meet their expectations for a happy old age. By planning now for your retirement, you stand a better chance of meeting your objectives.

Form 3-2

Expenses	Current	At retirement
Housing		
Property tax		
Insurance		
Utilities		
Maintenance		
Condo fees		
Other		
Food		
Clothing		
Transportation		
Car payments		
Insurance		
Fuel		
Maintenance		
Cab fare		
Public transit		
Phone		
Sundries (newspapers, magazines, books, cable TV, and so on)		
Recreation		
Self-improvement		
Medical, dental		
Life insurance		
Liability insurance		
Disability insurance		
Charitable contributions		
Total		

By determining the number of years until you retire and the average rate of inflation, you can determine how much you'll need if your spending remains at the same level in the future.

Table 1: Future Worth of One Dollar at the Beginning of the Year With Amount of Return Compounded Annually

					Annual Rate of Return							
Year	1%	2%	3%	4%	5%	6%	7%	8%	9%	10%	13%	15%
1	1.01	1.02	1.03	1.04	1.05	1.06	1.07	1.08	1.09	1.10	1.13	1.15
2	1.02	1.04	1.06	1.08	1.10	1.12	1.15	1.17	1.19	1.21	1.28	1.32
3	1.03	1.06	1.09	1.12	1.16	1.19	1.23	1.26	1.30	1.33	1.44	1.52
4	1.04	1.08	1.13	1.17	1.22	1.26	1.31	1.36	1.41	1.46	1.63	1.75
5	1.05	1.10	1.16	1.22	1.28	1.34	1.40	1.47	1.54	1.61	1.84	2.01
6	1.06	1.13	1.19	1.27	1.34	1.42	1.50	1.59	1.68	1.77	2.08	2.31
7	1.07	1.15	1.23	1.32	1.41	1.50	1.61	1.71	1.83	1.95	2.35	2.66
8	1.08	1.17	1.27	1.37	1.48	1.59	1.72	1.85	1.99	2.14	2.66	3.06
9	1.09	1.20	1.30	1.42	1.55	1.69	1.84	2.00	2.17	2.36	3.00	3.52
10	1.10	1.22	1.34	1.48	1.63	1.79	1.97	2.16	2.37	2.59	3.40	4.05
11	1.12	1.24	1.38	1.54	1.71	1.90	2.11	2.33	2.58	2.85	3.84	4.65
12	1.13	1.27	1.43	1.60	1.80	2.01	2.25	2.52	2.81	3.14	4.34	5.35
13	1.14	1.29	1.47	1.67	1.89	2.13	2.41	2.72	3.07	3.45	4.90	6.15
14	1.15	1.32	1.51	1.73	1.98	2.26	2.58	2.94	3.34	3.80	5.54	7.08
15	1.16	1.35	1.56	1.80	2.08	2.40	2.76	3.17	3.64	4.18	6.25	8.14
16	1.17	1.37	1.60	1.87	2.18	2.54	2.95	3.43	3.97	4.60	7.07	9.36
17	1.18	1.40	1.65	1.95	2.29	2.69	3.16	3.70	4.33	5.05	7.99	10.76
18	1.20	1.43	1.70	2.03	2.41	2.85	3.38	4.00	4.72	5.56	9.02	12.38

19	1.21	1.46	1.75	2.11	2.53	3.03	3.62	4.32	5.14	6.12	10.20	14.23
20	1.22	1.49	1.81	2.19	2.65	3.21	3.87	4.67	5.60	6.73	11.52	16.37
21	1.23	1.52	1.86	2.28	2.79	3.40	4.14	5.03	6.11	7.40	13.02	18.82
22	1.24	1.55	1.92	2.37	2.93	3.60	4.43	5.44	6.66	8.14	14.71	21.65
23	1.26	1.58	1.97	2.46	3.07	3.82	4.74	5.87	7.26	8.95	16.63	24.89
24	1.27	1.61	2.03	2.56	3.23	4.05	5.07	6.34	7.91	9.85	18.79	28.63
25	1.28	1.64	2.09	2.67	3.39	4.29	5.43	6.86	8.62	10.83	21.23	32.92
26	1.30	1.67	2.16	2.77	3.56	4.55	5.81	7.40	9.40	11.92	23.99	37.86
27	1.31	1.71	2.22	2.88	3.73	4.82	6.21	7.99	10.25	13.11	27.11	43.54
28	1.32	1.74	2.29	3.00	3.92	5.11	6.65	8.63	11.17	14.42	30.63	50.07
29	1.33	1.78	2.36	3.12	4.12	5.42	7.11	9.32	12.17	15.86	34.62	57.58
30	1.35	1.81	2.43	3.24	4.32	5.74	7.61	10.06	13.27	17.45	39.12	66.21
31	1.36	1.85	2.50	3.37	4.54	6.09	8.15	10.87	14.46	19.19	44.20	76.14
32	1.37	1.88	2.58	3.51	4.76	6.45	8.72	11.74	15.76	21.11	49.95	87.57
33	1.39	1.92	2.65	3.65	5.00	6.84	9.33	12.68	17.18	23.23	56.44	100.70
34	1.40	1.96	2.73	3.79	5.25	7.25	9.98	13.69	18.73	25.55	63.78	115.81
35	1.42	2.00	2.81	3.95	5.52	7.69	10.68	14.79	20.41	28.10	72.07	133.18
36	1.43	2.04	2.90	4.10	5.79	8.15	11.42	15.97	22.25	30.91	81.44	153.15
37	1.45	2.08	2.99	4.27	6.08	8.64	12.22	17.25	24.25	34.00	92.02	176.13
38	1.46	2.12	3.07	4.44	6.39	9.15	13.08	18.63	26.44	37.40	103.99	202.54
39	1.47	2.16	3.17	4.62	6.70	9.70	14.00	20.12	28.82	41.15	117.51	232.93
40	1.49	2.21	3.26	4.80	7.04	10.29	14.97	21.73	31.41	45.26	132.78	267.86

personal
financial vehicles

4

No matter how much you earn, you can always spend more. As your business becomes more successful, generating more money for you and your family after several years of effort, you might feel tempted to indulge yourself at long last in a few luxuries.

There's nothing wrong with rewarding yourself for your efforts, as long as you remember that you want to succeed in your personal financial life as well as in your business. Success always boils down to a single strategy: Spend less than you make.

Once you apply that simple rule, you can proceed to invest productively, as we'll explain in this chapter. But you first have to follow a disciplined investment plan instead of spending everything you make.

Unfortunately, most Canadians don't save their money, whether they're entrepreneurs, employees, students, or pensioners. Young people put off saving till they're older. Older people put off saving till they're married. Married people put off saving till the kids come along. Entrepreneurs put off saving till their business becomes firmly established. Parents put off saving till the kids grow up. And by then, the kids have spent it.

As a result, over 75% of Canadian men who reach age 65 are dead broke —or they never made any money at all. The statistics for women are even worse. Over 80% of women who reach age 65 require financial assistance. How many folks end up financially secure? About three in every hundred.

In another 25 years, the cost of living will probably double. If you're 55 or younger, you'll likely never see an old age security cheque. By the time you retire, the government will have taken it all back.

THE RULE OF 72

Once you invest it, your money will grow, thanks to the phenomenon of compound interest. Here's a handy way to remember how it works.

The number 72 is a magical number. Divide 72 by your annual investment return. You'll end up with the number of years it will take to double your money.

Say you earn 6% on your CSB. Divide 72 by 6. You get 12. It will take 12 years to double your money.

If you earn 20% on your money, you'll double it every 3.6 years.

CHOOSING YOUR INVESTMENTS

Your approach to investing, like your approach to business, depends on your personal likes and dislikes, attitudes, objectives, and tolerance for risk. Since you've already developed a personal financial plan, however, you've identified your objectives and your strategies for reaching them. Now comes the time to execute your personal financial plan.

You have a variety of investment instruments to choose from, ranging from CSBs to futures contracts. Your success depends on how well you understand your own objectives and needs and how well you understand your investment options.

A person who requires an income from his investments will choose a different strategy and different investment vehicles from one who wants to accumulate wealth for her retirement. Someone who wants to save money to buy a house will take a third approach.

1. SHORT-TERM SAVINGS

Do you know how much money you have in the bank? A surprising number of people don't. They let their money sit in a bank savings account instead of using their money to its best advantage, and theirs. Statistics show that there's more than one bank savings account open for every person in Canada. Obviously we're doing something wrong.

Savings accounts will never pay you enough money in interest to stay ahead of inflation. So you should use them only as a temporary storage place, while you decide what to do with your money.

Some savings accounts pay interest at a rate of 1/2% a year. At that rate, you'll double your money every 144 years.

Even among savings accounts, there are good ones and not so good ones.

In a conventional account, interest is tabulated monthly. Money deposited in a conventional savings account after the first day of the month doesn't earn interest for the entire month.

In a daily interest account, money in the account earns interest on the first day that you deposit it and every day after that, until you remove it. Even if you leave it there for only one day, it will still earn interest, at a slightly lower rate than it would earn in a conventional savings account.

The difference in interest income on money held in a savings account may not seem like a lot, but it could cover the cost of a couple of CDs or an extra Christmas present, especially if you pay yourself at regular intervals. Say you pay yourself every two weeks, and your take-home pay is around $900. If you deposit your cheque into a daily interest account earning 2 1/2% annually, and if you can leave your cheque in the account for only eight days, you'll earn about 70¢; 26 times each year. That comes to an extra $18 to $20 each year. You get this money for doing nothing more than opening a daily interest savings account rather than a conventional savings account.

DEPOSIT INSURANCE

Keeping your money in Canadian banks, trust companies, or credit unions is very safe. Any institution that displays the Canadian Deposit Insurance Corporation (CDIC) sticker provides guaranteed protection of all funds deposited up to $60,000.

This means any money that you hold in a savings account, chequing account, GIC, or term deposit is guaranteed up to $60,000 *per institution*, not per branch. If you have over $60,000 sitting in a bank, you can get around the guaranteed limit by keeping up to $60,000 in your name, up to $60,000 in your spouse's name, up to $60,000 in a joint account and up to $60,000 in an RRSP, all within the same institution and all guaranteed.

CDIC coverage does not extend to credit unions. However, provincial deposit insurance programs can provide them with insurance coverage of customer accounts up to $60,000 apiece. Many credit unions also allow clients to keep as many RRSPs as they want, guaranteeing the funds in each of them up to $60,000.

THE SLUSH FUND

In general, cash doesn't provide a big return, no matter where you keep it. No one will pay you much for the use of your cash today, if you can take it back again with no explanation tomorrow.

Nevertheless, you should set aside between 10% and 50% of your investment holdings in cash-type investments as a slush fund. The slush fund provides flexibility, liquidity, and peace of mind. If the value of your other investments falls drastically, you can still resort to your slush fund for ready cash to take advantage of other opportunities. Following a buy-low, sell-high strategy, you'll always need some cash to take advantage of lower prices in other investment areas.

You can keep your cash relatively handy in deposit accounts, term deposits, GICs, CSBs, and mortgage-backed securities. Treasury bills,

Canadian money market funds, and international money funds are also useful, but slightly less accessible.

The Deposit Account

High-interest savings accounts may also be called a premium account, investor account, or cash performance account. These accounts provide a higher interest rate than a conventional savings account. Many institutions require a hefty deposit of at least $25,000 to get a piece of the action. Also, these deposit accounts come with only limited cheque-writing privileges, restrictions on withdrawals, and a variable, not fixed, interest rate. In other words, the account may pay 4% when you deposit your money, but there's no guarantee that the interest rate won't drop.

Term Deposits

A term deposit is a short-term contract between you and the financial institution, extending for thirty days to one year, although some term deposits can extend over five years. Under the contract, you lend your money to the financial institution for a specified period. In return, the financial institution pays you a fixed rate of interest until the contract expires. In general, the longer the term, the higher the interest rate. Sometimes the interest rate on a term deposit is less than the rate on a premium savings account offered by banks. Also, you can cancel a term deposit prior to maturity, but only if you pay a penalty charge.

GICs

GICs are similar to term deposits. But GICs usually have longer terms, maturing in one year or more. Since your money is tied up for a fixed period, only the shortest-term GICs can be considered liquid investments. Most GICs lock up your money for the duration of the contract. Some financial institutions, however, will allow you to cash in a GIC early, if you pay a penalty.

To protect yourself against interest-rate swings, you can buy five GICs of equal value, with staggered maturity dates. For instance, if you have $5,000 to invest, you should buy

• A one-year GIC for $1000,

- A two-year GIC for $1000,
- A three-year GIC for $1000,
- A four-year GIC for $1000, and
- A five-year GIC for $1000.

After the first year

- The one-year GIC will mature.
- The two-year GIC will now have one year left until maturity.
- The three-year GIC will now have two years left until maturity.
- The four-year GIC will now have three years left until maturity.
- The five-year GIC will now have four years left until maturity.

As your GIC matures each year, you should reinvest the proceeds in a new five-year GIC, to replace your most recent five-year GIC, which now has only four years left until it matures.

Follow this strategy year after year. No matter what happens, one GIC will mature every year, and you'll continually reinvest the money at the current interest rate.

Canada Savings Bonds

CSBs are one of the most popular savings instruments. Each fall, CSBs are sold through financial institutions like banks and trust companies to Canadian residents. They come in denominations of $100, $300, $500, $1000, $5000, and $10,000. Currently the limit on the total value of CSBs that you can purchase in one year is $100,000. Purchasers can choose bonds that pay regular or compound interest. Interest rates for CSBs are set each year when they're issued, and are guaranteed for only one year. Each year, the CSB yield may stay the same or go up or down, depending upon the current economic climate.

The advantages of CSBs are:

- They're easy to purchase.
- They're extremely safe.
- They're highly liquid, which means you can always find someone to take them off your hands if you want to cash them.

The disadvantages of CSBs are:

- They must be held for at least three months before you can collect any accrued interest.
- When your CSB matures after one year and you use the money to buy another CSB, you can't predict the interest rate that will prevail at the time.

CSBs do not respond like conventional bonds to interest-rate swings. No matter how high or how low rates go, you can always cash in your CSB and get your full investment back, even if you cash it in before it matures. That's because the government guarantees the full value of CSBs.

Because there's so little risk associated with CSBs, no one pays a premium or a discount to buy them. The only risk associated with a CSB comes from inflation.

T-Bills

The Canadian government regularly needs to borrow enormous amounts of money for short periods. Once a week, it sells Treasury Bills in an auction to banks and other large financial institutions. Treasury Bills are actually very short-term bonds backed by the Canadian government. They mature in three months, six months, or one year. They're among the safest investments in the world. And there's a huge market for them, which makes them very easy to buy and sell.

Mortgage-Backed Securities

Mortgage-backed securities (MBSs) are pools of high-grade residential mortgages. Financial institutions put together hundreds of mortgages into a single package, called a pool. Then they sell shares in the pool to investors like you. Theoretically, you're lending your money to a borrower whose mortgage is in the pool. The financial institution is acting as an intermediary.

Each pool comes with its own interest rate and payment schedule. If a mortgage borrower defaults on a mortgage in the pool, you don't lose your money. That's because the interest and principal of the mortgage are both guaranteed by the Canada Mortgage and Housing Corporation (CMHC).

Theoretically, there's a correlation between the dollars lent in the form of mortgages and the dollars borrowed from investors in MBSs.

An investment in an MBS

- Pays an above-average yield,
- Provides regular cash flow,
- Is government-guaranteed, and
- Is guaranteed regardless of the amount contributed.

You'll need at least $5,000 to purchase an MBS. MBSs can be purchased from brokers, and are issued by banks and trust companies that hold mortgages. Most are issued with five-year terms and can be held in an RRSP or an RRIF.

The interest rate that you receive from an MBS depends upon the interest charged to the mortgage holders. The financial institution calculates the lowest mortgage rate of all the mortgages in the pool. Then it pays MBS investors one half point below the lowest rate.

If you want to cash in your MBS before it matures, you can sell it relatively easily on the secondary market. However, if you sell the MBS before it matures, the amount you receive will depend on the current interest rate. When interest rates rise, your MBS will fall in value; when interest rates fall, your MBS will rise in value.

The best time to buy an MBS is when interest rates are high and beginning to fall. That way, you can sell it before it matures for a profit on your original investment. However, if you plan on holding your MBS until it matures, any time is a good time to purchase one.

2. LONGER-TERM INVESTMENTS: BONDS

A bond is basically a promissory note that explains when a borrower will repay your money and at what rate of interest. Bonds are sold by governments and corporations. They're big, stable, conservative, and reliable, and they usually repay their debts. (This isn't always the case, though, so you shouldn't make assumptions. Investigate your investments.)

Bondholders are lenders, not owners. Unlike a shareholder, a company's bondholders do not share in the company's growth. They receive no dividends, and their capital gains are not related to the rise or fall of the company's stock price. However, a corporation is legally obligated to repay its loans from its bondholders whether it makes a profit or not. If it cannot meet its payments, the bondholders can force the firm into bankruptcy.

The face value or principal amount describes the amount of the bond to be repaid. The coupon rate is the rate of interest paid annually on a bond. The maturity date is the date when the bond matures and you receive your loan back.

Usually interest is paid twice a year, at a fixed rate. On the date when the entire amount has to be repaid—called the maturity date—you will receive back the bond's face value. The performance of the bond market is closely tied to movements in interest rates.

A bond consists of two parts: A piece of paper, which is the actual bond (also called the residual), and a number of smaller pieces of paper, called coupons.

At one time, you physically received your bond certificates with the coupons attached. To collect your interest, you just cut off a coupon and cashed it in every six months or so. Today it's largely done electronically.

A bond's annual interest rate is also called its coupon rate. In most cases, a bond's coupon rate is fixed for the duration of the term.

Once bonds start trading on the open market, their price is quoted at 1/10 of their actual price. For instance, if a bond sells at par for $1,000, then it will be listed in the newspaper as 100. If the bond sells at a premium for $1,200, then it will be listed as 120. If the bond sells at a discount for $850, then it will be listed as 85.

UPS AND DOWNS

When interest rates rise, the price of bonds falls. When interest rates fall, the price of bonds rises.

More specifically, when the prime rate rises by 1%, bond prices fall about 10%. When the prime rate falls 1%, bond prices rise about 10%.

Here's why: In January 1993, a corporation issues a $1,000 bond that matures in 30 years with an interest rate of 10%. Meanwhile, other corporations are issuing bonds at similar rates for 20 years or 10 years or even 40 years. If you buy the 30-year bond, you agree to lend this corporation $1,000. In return, the corporation promises to pay you 10% a year on your

$1,000 investment, for a total of 30 years. After 30 years, the corporation will pay you back your $1,000 in full.

In the year 2003, 10 years after you buy the bond, you decide you no longer want to keep it. Your bond is now 10 years old. It's no longer a 30-year bond. It's now a 20-year bond.

You originally paid $1,000 for it. But because money is harder to borrow in the year 2003, companies are issuing 20-year bonds with an interest rate of 12%. Your bond also matures in 20 years, but pays only 10% in interest.

As a result, you'll have to sell your bond for less than $1,000 to compensate the buyer for taking an interest rate of only 10%. In fact, you'll get about $830 for it.

On the other hand, if interest rates have fallen to 8% in 2003, your bond will increase in value, because it pays 10%. Instead of selling at the bond's face value of $1,000, you can sell it for about $1,250.

RISE AND FALL

When interest rates rise, bond prices fall. The extent of the decline is related to the bond's term to maturity. With a 2% rise in interest rates, a three-year bond will fall 5% in value. A 10-year bond will fall 12% in value. A 30-year bond will fall 18% in value.

YIELD

When a bond is first issued, the yield is usually set at a fixed rate for the life of the bond. That fixed interest rate is based on prevailing economic conditions.

Once a bond starts trading on the open market, its current yield is constantly adjusted to keep it competitive with other bonds.

The current yield is calculated by dividing the bond's coupon rate by the bond's current price. For example: When sold at par, a bond with a face value of $1,000 that pays a coupon rate of 8% ($80) will provide a current yield of $80/$1000, or 8%. If the bond's price rises to $1,100, its current yield will be $80/$1,100, or 7.3%. If the bond's price falls to $900, its current yield will be $80/$900, or 8.8%.

If you buy a bond at a discount, you'll have a capital gain when the bond matures and you collect its face value. The capital gain is equivalent to the difference between the price you pay for the bond and its face value.

For instance, if you buy a bond with a face value of $1,000, and you pay only $900, you'll have a capital gain of $100 when the bond matures. The yield to maturity involves comparing the capital gain with the years to maturity to arrive at the actual purchase price. When you look at bond tables in the financial pages, the column showing the yield represents the yield to maturity.

When a bond is purchased at a discount, the yield to maturity will be higher than the current yield. When a bond is purchased at a premium, the yield to maturity will be less than the current yield.

CALLING ALL BONDS

Most bonds are issued with a provision known as a call. A call gives the bond issuer the right to call in the bond before it matures.

This might happen if interest rates fall. Say a company issues bonds in 1995 yielding 10%. In 1998, interest rates fall to 8%. If the corporation can call in its old 10% bonds and replace them with new 8% bonds, it will save itself 2% in annual interest payments.

In return for calling the bond, the corporation will usually pay the bondholder a premium above the bond's face value, usually equal to a year's interest. If you originally paid $1,000 for a bond paying 10%, the issuer would likely pay you about $1,100 to call it back before it matured.

Most bonds cannot be called in at least for the first five or six years after they're issued.

BOND RATINGS

Bond issuers pay interest for the privilege of borrowing your money and also to compensate you for your risk. The lower a bond's rating, the higher the interest paid by the issuer.

To measure the risk of investing in a bond, investors rely on credit ratings. The credit rating of a company or government reflects its stability and trustworthiness. The higher the rating, the lower the risk and the safer the bond.

Bond rating services in Canada include Dominion Bond Rating Service (DBRS), Canadian Bond Rating Service (CBRS), Standard & Poor's, and Moody's Investor Service. Your broker can tell you the rating for any bond that interests you.

BOND VARIATIONS

Nothing is simple in the world of bonds. Corporations and investment dealers have developed a variety of instruments based on bonds to attract investors. Here are a few.

Convertible Bonds

To make their bonds more attractive to investors, many corporations offer convertible bonds. These give the bondholders the privilege of converting their bonds into a specified number of the company's common shares at a specific conversion price.

These bonds still carry all the features of regular bonds, such as coupon rate, face value, maturity date, and call date. But because they're closely tied to the company's common stock, their price rises and falls in relation to the stock price. When the common stock rises in value, so does the price of the convertible bond.

The performance of these bonds is much more volatile than regular bonds. Convertibles also tend to carry lower yields than regular bonds.

Debentures

Debentures are a type of bond issued frequently by large industrial corporations. They're not backed by real estate or property that can be sold to repay the bondholders if the company goes under. Instead, they're backed only by the general credit of the corporation.

First Mortgage Bonds

These bonds are backed by a first mortgage on the company's property. They offer investors first claim on the company's assets if it defaults on the repayment of its loan. They're generally quite safe.

Strip Bonds

Before you go to the bank or the trust company to reinvest a GIC or CSB that reaches maturity, you have no guarantee that the new interest rate will be as good as your current one. One way to obtain such a guarantee is to buy a strip-coupon bond. It will let you know exactly what you'll earn this year, next year, and every year until the bond matures.

Say your typical long-term government bond has a face value of $100,000, a 20-year term to maturity, a 10% yield, and coupons that pay $500 in interest, every six months. Instead of selling these bonds intact, brokerage firms buy them and separate the coupons from the rest of the bond. Now they can sell either the bond without the coupons or the coupons without the bond.

If you buy a bond without the coupons, you won't earn any interest. To compensate the investor, strip coupon bonds sell at a discount. Instead of paying the full face value for a $100,000 bond, for example, you pay about $15,000.

When the stripped bond matures 20 years down the road, you can cash it in and collect the face value—$100,000. That's $85,000 more than you paid for it, which represents your earned interest.

Strip coupon bonds offer several advantages:

1. When rates are high, you can lock your money away to earn high yields year after year.
2. Once you buy a strip, you can forget about it till it matures.
3. You have no more worries about reinvesting your money at lower rates.
4. You're buying the bond at a discount, so you don't need a lot of money to invest up front.
5. You know exactly how much money you'll have when the strip matures.

TAX ISSUES

Even though you won't receive any money until the strip matures, Revenue Canada will tax you each year on the interest. That's why the best place to hold your strip bonds is inside a tax-free account such as an RRSP or RRIF.

BOND FUNDS

Rather than investing with the aim of increasing the value of their holdings, bond funds focus on income, usually investing in government, corporate, and strip-coupon bonds.

Like individual bonds, bond mutual funds respond to interest rates. When interest rates rise, bond mutual funds fall in value. When interest rates fall, bond mutual funds rise in value.

The price fluctuation (volatility) of a particular bond fund is directly proportional to the average maturity of all the bonds held in the fund's portfolio. The longer it takes for its bond-holdings to mature, the more sensitive the bond fund will be to changes in interest rates.

In general, funds that invest primarily in long-term bonds (maturing in 20 to 25 years) will be more volatile than funds that invest primarily in intermediate-term bonds (maturing in five to ten years).

A short-term bond fund that invests primarily in bonds maturing in one to three years will be the least volatile.

FOREIGN BOND FUNDS

The Canadian bond market represents only 4% of the world's government bond market. So if you're limiting your bond investments solely to Canada, you may be missing out. Here's what foreign bonds recently earned compared to Canadian bonds.

- 1986: Japanese bonds earn 37%, Canadian bonds earn 13%.
- 1987: United Kingdom bonds earn 35%, Canadian bonds earn 3%.
- 1988: Australian bonds earn 18%, Canadian bonds earn 9%.
- 1989: Canadian bonds are the top performers, earning around 13%.
- 1990: United Kingdom bonds earn 23%, Canadian bonds earn 20%.
- 1991: Australian bonds earn 23%, Canadian bonds earn 20%.

Before you can purchase another country's bonds, you must convert your money into that country's currency. For instance, if you want to purchase German bonds, you must first convert your Canadian dollars into German marks.

That doesn't guarantee a profit, even if you're right on your timing, and German bonds appreciate in value. The mark could fall in value faster than the Canadian dollar. So when you sell your German bonds for marks, then use the marks to buy Canadian dollars, you end up with fewer dollars than you started with.

This is called currency risk. To counter currency risk, some global funds hedge their bets by buying less volatile currencies.

A fund manager purchasing German bonds, for example, would sell marks on the foreign exchange market and buy a currency that will not fall so much in value, such as the U.S. dollar. The result is a currency-hedged German bond position.

This type of fund is much less volatile than a non-hedged bond fund. However, because of the hedging, their potential profits are lower than non-hedged funds.

INVESTMENT TIP

Never invest in bond mutual funds when interest rates are rising. And if you've already invested in a bond fund, sell.

THE LONG-TERM VIEW

Over the past seven decades, bonds have returned average annual gains of less than 5%. Yet many investors still believe the best strategy is to hold on to their bonds until they mature, regardless of the direction of interest rates. After all, they reason, no matter which way interest rates go, they'll still continue to receive their interest payments. And when the bond matures, they'll get its full face value.

When interest rates are declining, that rationale makes sense. But when interest rates rise, bondholders lose. There's no doubt about it. That's because they lose the opportunity to invest their money in new, higher-yielding bonds.

Rising interest rates mean lower bond prices. Falling rates mean higher bond prices. So we should buy bonds when interest rates reach a peak and begin to decline. We should sell bonds when interest rates hit bottom and begin to rise.

In fact, you should never buy bonds unless interest rates are high. That's the cardinal rule of the bond market.

An effective way to decide how much of your portfolio to invest in bonds is to use your age as a guideline.

- **Age 34 or younger: 5% in bonds or bond funds**
- **Age 35 to 49: 15% in bonds or bond funds**
- **Age 49 and up: 30% in bonds or bond funds**

INVESTMENT BAROMETER

Over the past 80 years, the bond market has always undergone a major downturn either before or at the same time as every major downturn in the stock market. At the end of each of the last six recessions, when the stock market reached bottom, bonds began rising an average of four months prior to stocks.

What ties the two markets together? Interest rates. The very thought of rising interest rates sends shivers up the spines of many bond holders. As interest rates rise, people pull their money out of the stock market and put it into GICs yielding double-digit returns. Thus, when bonds turn, stocks follow the leader and turn, too.

3. LONGER-TERM INVESTMENTS: EQUITIES

With an equity investment, you become an owner, not a lender. You might invest in shares of a company, gold, corn, or antique furniture. Equity investments provide a return based on the increase in the value of the share or property. Public corporations may also pay shareholders a percentage of company profits in the form of dividends on their shares.

Over long periods, a diversified portfolio of equity investments has historically generated higher returns than all other investments. Over short periods, however, they can perform erratically. Since you've already determined your capacity for risk, you can incorporate equities into your investment portfolio accordingly.

Share prices respond to factors such as a company's financial performance and management, its future prospects, and the general state of the economy. In general, the greater the risk, the greater the volatility and the greater the potential rewards.

COMMON STOCK

Public companies trade their shares on stock exchanges around the world. The majority of shares on the market are common stocks. As a holder of common stock, you can participate in a company's growth by electing its board of directors, voting on corporate policies, and attending its annual meetings. Common stocks provide investment returns through the increase in the value of the stock and through income from dividends. The size of a dividend generally reflects the company's performance.

Public companies have to follow rules, set by securities regulators, such as publishing an annual report, reporting insider trades, and so on, that aim to prevent unscrupulous companies from taking the public's money unfairly. Private companies can sell shares as well, but they can't sell them to the general public.

The shares of public companies are traded all day, five days a week, on one or more of Canada's three major stock exchanges.

- The Toronto Stock Exchange (TSE) is the largest and best known.
- The Montreal Exchange (ME) is a big player in certain areas such as futures and options.
- The Vancouver Stock Exchange (VSE) specializes in low-priced, more speculative stocks, including a lot of mining stocks.

There's also a stock exchange in Alberta (the Alberta Exchange), and a commodities exchange in Winnipeg.

EVALUATING STOCKS

Investors look more closely at a company's earnings per share than at any other financial figure. A company calculates its earnings per share by dividing its net earnings by the number of shares outstanding.

For example, if a company has net earnings of $100 million, and it has 20 million shares outstanding, then the earnings per share are $5 ($100 million ÷ 20 million = $5).

There are two calculations to determine the value of a stock: the price/earnings ratio, and the dividend yield.

Also called the P/E ratio or P/E multiple, the Price/Earnings ratio measures the current price of the share in relationship to the earnings per share. It is calculated by dividing the current share price by the last 12 months' earnings per share.

If a company's stock is trading at $30 a share, and the company earns $2 a share, the P/E ratio would be 15 ($30 ÷ $2 = 15).

The ratio of price to earnings indicates the premium that an investor will pay to own a piece of the company. A P/E ratio of 15 indicates that an investor will pay 15 times as much as the company earns in a year to own a share. Investors figure the company will grow and that they will recover their investment in less than 15 years.

The P/E ratio tells us how much the stock could potentially grow. The higher a company's potential for growth, the more value the market places on its stock. A P/E ratio of 20 indicates that investors will pay the equivalent of 20 years of profits for the stock. A P/E ratio of 40 means the market is much more optimistic about the company's growth prospects and will pay the equivalent of 40 years of profits for a share.

The market doesn't expect to wait for 40 years to get its money back. It expects the company to grow so quickly that it will recover its investment in a much shorter time. Sometimes the market is right. Sometimes it's not.

A low P/E ratio implies that a company has low potential for growth. It also tells us how much risk is associated with the stock. The market may not expect much growth from a company whose stock has a low P/E ratio. But it also doesn't see much risk in investing in the company. So its stock price will remain relatively stable.

When the stock market turns down, the stocks that decline furthest in price are the ones with high P/E ratios. As a general rule, stocks that have a P/E ratio above 30 represent a higher risk.

A large decline in the P/E ratio of a company's stock is a warning sign. It indicates that all may not be well with the company. For example, if a stock's P/E ratio falls from 30 to 20 in less than a year, investors have lost confidence in the stock.

Dividend yield represents a stock's indicated dividend for the next 12 months divided by the current share price. The dividend yield indicates the annual return that an investor receives from a stock's dividends. It lets you compare the annual return on different kinds of investments.

The yield from your savings account may be 3%, for example. The dividend yield from your shares in a company might be 2 1/2%. However, as we'll see, yield isn't everything.

If a company pays its stockholders a cash dividend of 50¢, and the share price is currently $20, then the dividend yield will be 2 1/2%. (Remember, divide the dividend by the share price and multiply by 100.)

Some people invest in safe secure companies whose stock has a low P/E ratio but a relatively high dividend yield. These companies may not grow quickly, but they won't go down the tubes next week.

Other people invest in more risky stocks with high P/E ratios but low dividend yields. These companies may grow so fast that their stock will double in value overnight, if they don't go out of business altogether.

DIVIDENDS

A company that passes all its profits to shareholders in the form of high dividends may not last long. To compete with other companies, a business has to reinvest at least some of its profits in buildings, equipment, employees, and expansion. It can't give all its profits to its shareholders.

MARKET INDEX

A market index like the TSE 300 measures the general performance of specific and usually reliable stocks. The TSE 300, for example, is based on the value of 300 stocks trading on the Toronto Stock Exchange.

The index began in 1977, when the total value of all 300 stocks was $34 billion. Rather than juggle all those zeroes, the TSE allotted an arbitrary number of 1,000 to represent the value of the TSE 300 at that time. Since then, every time the value of shares represented by the TSE 300 Composite Index rose $3.4 million from the previous day's value, the index itself rose by one point. So the news announcer would say, for example, that the TSE rose one point today, to 1,001.

A market index represents a general market movement, not the movement of individual stocks. The TSE index would have to rise 45 points for the value of those 300 companies to increase by 1%. But even if the TSE 300 rose by 45 points, it would not mean that the value of each of those 300 companies increased by 1% as well. Some may have gone up 2%, others only 1/2%. And others may have lost 2%.

In the U.S., the most popular market index is the Dow Jones Industrial Average—the Dow. Started by Charles H. Dow in 1896, the index originally included only 12 stocks. On the first day of trading, the Dow Industrials closed at 40.94. Today the Dow Industrials contain 30 stocks, and the index is currently around 6,000.

For people who think the Dow, with only 30 stocks, can't possibly reflect accurately the activity of the entire U.S. stock market, there's Standard & Poor's 500 Index—the S&P 500. It's based on the ups and downs of 500 large U.S. industrial stocks.

READING THE TABLES
Everything you need to know about a company's day-to-day financial performance you can find in the stock tables. You just have to know how to read them. Here's how.

Figure 4-1

52 Weeks						Yld	Vol				Net
Hi	Lo	Stock	Sym	Div	%	100s	Hi	Lo	Close	Chg
50⅜	42	BCE Inc	B	2.68	5.4	21680	50⅜	49⅛	50⅛	+1⅛

- Hi and Lo: These show the highest and the lowest price at which the stock traded over the previous 52 weeks.
- Stock: This is the name of the company whose stock you're viewing.
- Sym: This is the symbol that represents BCE's stock on the ticker. (You can see the ticker in action in brokerage offices.)
- Div: This is the company's estimated annual dividend per share.
- Yld %: This is the stock's dividend yield.
- Vol 100s: This is the number of shares that have been traded throughout the day.

- The last few columns represent the highest price throughout the day, the lowest price throughout the day, the closing price at the end of the day, and the percent change from the previous day.

BID AND ASK

A stock may have an ask price of $10 and a bid of 9 3/4. If you wanted to sell the stock right away, you'd have to accept the bid price of $9.75. If you wanted to buy the stock right away, you'd have to pay the ask price of $10.

You can also place an order to buy or sell a stock at a price in between the bid and ask, at 9 7/8. But if you do, there's no guarantee that your order will get filled.

Bid and ask prices are constantly changing in relation to supply and demand.

The standard unit in which stocks are bought and sold is 100 shares. Just as eggs are sold by the dozen, shares are sold by the board lot: 100 shares per board lot. For stocks trading over $1, the bid and ask prices are quoted per board lot. A purchase of under 100 shares is known as an odd lot.

There are three ways to place an order with a stockbroker:

1. A market order: You want to buy a particular stock at the current market price. For example, let's say you want to buy 100 shares of BCE Inc. You would call up your stockbroker and say, "What's BCE trading at?" She'll say, "50 bid, 50 1/4 ask." If you find this range attractive, you say, "Buy 100 shares of BCE at the market." Your broker will repeat the order to you and then place it. You now own 100 shares of BCE at 50 1/4.

2. A limit order: You want to buy or sell a stock only if it trades at a specified price. You also have to set a time limit for your order. You could set the time limit for one day, one month, or any duration in between. Or you could place an order "good till cancelled," in which case the order stays in effect until it's either executed or cancelled by you.

   For example, if BCE is trading at $50, but you don't want to pay more than $48 for it, you would tell your broker to "Buy BCE at $48, good for the week." At the end of one week, if the trade isn't executed, it's automatically cancelled.

3. A stop order: You want to sell a stock whose price has gone up and is now starting to fall. So you instruct your broker: "Place a stop order."

For example, if you bought a stock at $20, it rose to $40, and it's now starting to head lower—$39...$38...$37...you don't want to lose your profits. So you phone your broker and say, "Place a stop order to sell 100 shares at $35." Now if the stock drops to $35, your shares will automatically be sold.

NO GUARANTEES

Over the long term, the average stock price rises by 10% to 12% a year. But the prices of individual stocks do not always follow that average. The price of a stock can fall so quickly, it will eliminate gains accumulated over the entire previous year. With this in mind, you should not regard individual stocks as long-term investments. Instead, think of them as trading vehicles. Once you've made a substantial profit on a particular stock, sell it.

STOCK SELECTION

The most important factor for picking a winning stock is an increase in the company's earnings per share.

Buy a stock only if it records an increase in earnings per share in the most recent quarter compared to the same quarter last year. Yearly earnings are also very important. Top-performing stocks should have at least a four-year to five-year track record of back-to-back increases in annual earnings per share.

However, the key rule to follow in conducting your personal and business financial affairs remains: Don't put all your eggs in one basket.

About 75% of stocks follow the general stock-market trend. The other 25% march to a different drummer. The challenge is to figure out which are which, so you can get in at the bottom and ride a stock to the top, rather than getting in at the bottom just as the bottom falls out.

"Don't put all your eggs in one basket" is also called asset allocation. Asset allocation means you always put some of your money in cash, some in income-producing investments, and some in stocks or stock funds. If a bear market comes along, you can limit your losses.

SELLING SHORT

When you buy a stock hoping that it will rise in value, you are said to be investing long. If you think the price of the stock will fall, you can sell short.

Instead of buying a stock and then selling it, short sellers sell a stock, then buy it back later, when the price is lower (they hope). They do this by borrowing stock through a brokerage firm, then selling it at the current market price. If they've predicted correctly, they go out and repurchase the stock at a lower price. They return the shares to the original lender and keep the difference in price. Sometimes short sellers are wrong, and the stock's price rises. Then the short seller has to buy back the shares at a higher price and suffer a loss.

PREFERRED SHARES

Preferred shares pay fixed dividends at regular intervals, usually quarterly and usually at a higher rate than common shares. Like bonds, preferred shares depend for their value on the level of market interest rates and the creditworthiness of the corporate issuer. When interest rates rise, the price of preferred stocks fall. Similarly, when interest rates fall, preferred stocks rise.

Preferred shares usually don't carry voting rights. But if the company is liquidated, the rights of preferred shareholders take precedence over the rights of the owners of common stock, although they come behind the rights attached to bonds, debentures, and most other creditors.

The creditworthiness of preferred shares also depends on the features and conditions of the shares themselves. Some of these favour the investor and some the company.

Cumulative Dividends

If dividend payments are suspended or reduced, and then the company's fortunes improve, preferred shareholders must receive all the unpaid dividends before the company can pay dividends on its common shares.

Fixed Retraction

The company commits to redeeming the shares at the issue price or par value, on a set date in the future. Alternatively, the shares may be redeemed at the investor's option, at a set price and after a set date in the future.

Convertibility

When convertible preferreds are issued, the conversion price is usually above the market price of the common stock. Investors buy them because they pay dividends at a higher rate than the common stock. Over time, however, the common stock price may rise, and the conversion feature becomes increasingly valuable. The holder of a convertible preferred share can convert it at any time into a specified number of common shares. Say a company sells its convertible preferred shares for $100 each. A conversion clause allows you to convert each convertible preferred share into 10 shares of the company's common stock at any time within the next five years. At the time, its common stock is trading at $9 a share. Since 10 shares at $9 apiece are worth $90, there's no benefit in exercising the conversion clause at current prices. But when the price of a common share rises above $10, then it makes sense to convert. For example, if the price of a common share rises to $12, you can convert your convertible preferred, for which you paid $100, into 10 common shares, and get $120.

Call Feature

Often, convertible securities come with a redemption clause allowing the company to redeem them at their face value after a certain period. If, at this time, the common share price is higher than the conversion price, a call for redemption will force investors to convert their securities.

WHEN TO BUY PREFERREDS

Unlike regular preferreds, the convertible's price tends to move in line with the price of the common stock. This can be good or bad, depending upon which way the common stock moves.

It is best to buy preferred stock when interest rates have peaked and are beginning to decline. At that time, dividend payouts will be high, and stock prices low.

You should also consider purchasing convertible preferred shares during periods of rising inflation. When inflation is low, the fixed payment that you receive from the
dividend on your preferred share retains its value. But when
inflation rises, it erodes the value of your dividend payment.
If you convert the shares to common stock, the value of
your shares may go up, and the money you make in the
process won't be so vulnerable to the ravages of inflation.

FUTURES AND OPTIONS

Futures and options are also called derivative securities. For a corporation,
their primary function is to control risk. Some derivatives are traded
through exchanges; others are traded over the counter.

A future is simply a contract to buy or sell something, entered into now
for settlement at some future date. From an investment point of view, buying a future is the same as buying the underlying financial asset at its current price and paying for it with borrowed money. If the value of the
underlying asset goes up in the meantime, the difference between the increase and the contracted amount you pay for it represents your profit. So
the value of your future contract will rise as the value of the underlying
asset rises.

Futures reduce risk if they are part of a well-planned investment strategy. Suppose you have sold your home and intend to invest the proceeds
in gold on the closing date. If interest rates may drop before you close, gold
prices may rise. You can reduce your exposure by buying gold futures now
and selling them when the sale of your house closes. If gold prices actually rise, the profit on your futures will offset the higher cost of buying the
gold. If gold prices fall, you'll lose money on the futures, but your gold will
cost less as well. You can use the same technique for picking stocks or buying bonds.

An option gives an investor the right, but not the obligation, to buy
(call) or sell (put) specific assets for a fixed price within a specified time
frame. The price of an option depends on the current price of the underlying asset, the transaction (strike) price specified in the option, and the
length of time before it expires. The price volatility of the underlying asset,

the level of short-term interest rates, and the timing and size of dividends or other income also affect an option's price.

Like futures, options can be used to reduce risk. They're traded on exchanges, and you can buy them on equities and commodities.

PRECIOUS METALS AND COMMODITIES

These are highly speculative and should represent only a small portion of your investment portfolio. They're subject to an infinite number of forces, from global economic conditions and political changes to the price of wheat in Bulgaria. Precious metals can be purchased from banks and investment dealers as actual bullion or in the form of ownership certificates. Commodities such as grain, non-precious metals, and foods can be purchased from commodities exchanges in Winnipeg, Chicago, and elsewhere.

MUTUAL FUNDS

Most entrepreneurs have little time to spend managing their investment portfolios, especially in the initial stages of their business. While they should know how financial markets work, they don't necessarily have the time, talent, or inclination to manage their own investments.

As an alternative, you can hire a knowledgeable professional money manager to make informed decisions about where to invest your money and when. That's essentially what you get by investing in a mutual fund.

Mutual funds allow you to put your financial eggs in more than one basket, even if your portfolio is relatively small. So you can enjoy the same benefits of diversification as investors with more money. The mutual fund takes your money and pools it together with money from many other investors. Along with their money, the mutual fund manager can invest in a broad range of stocks, bonds, or other instruments.

In Canada, mutual fund companies must register with the provincial securities commission. In the U.S., mutual fund companies must register with the Securities and Exchange Commission. In either case, they're well-regulated, and their managers are well-qualified to make investments on their funds' behalf.

Major banks sell their own mutual funds. But many trust companies, insurance companies, and private companies sell mutual funds as well. In fact, there are hundreds of private companies to choose from. They have names like Altamira, Trimark, Bolton Tremblay, AGF, Templeton, and 20/20.

You often can't buy a private company's mutual fund (Templeton, Trimark, and so on) at your local bank. Similarly, you can't buy your favourite bank's mutual fund through a private company like Templeton or Trimark. They're all competing for your money. So compare them and choose the one that suits you.

OPEN OR CLOSED

Most mutual funds currently traded in Canada are open-ended. If you own shares in an open-ended mutual fund, you'll almost never have trouble finding someone to buy your shares or sell you more shares.

A few are closed-end mutual funds. These funds issue a limited number of shares when they're first set up. Once they sell all the shares, the fund is closed. At that point, no new shares are issued.

That's where the stock exchange comes in. You can still buy and sell shares in a closed-end fund on the stock exchange. The price will fluctuate, just like shares in other companies. Sometimes the price per share will sell at a premium. Sometimes it will sell at a discount.

Here's a typical listing of a closed-end fund:

Figure 4-2

Fund Name	Stock exchange	NAV	Market price	Premium discount
Korea Fund	NY	$10.14	$13.50	+33.1%

Here's what it all means.

- Shares in the Korea Fund are traded on the New York Stock Exchange.
- The current net asset value (NAV) is $10.14.
- If this were an open-ended fund, you would pay just $10.14 a share. But this is a closed-end fund. So you'll have to pay the market price: $13.50.
- Shares in the Korea Fund currently sell at a premium of 33.1% to its NAV. In other words, its $13.50-per-share price tag is 33.1% more than the NAV of $10.14.

LOAD AND NO-LOAD

Fund companies commonly charge a commission on the shares they sell. This commission is also called a load. The commission compensates the fund company, financial planner, and stockbroker for providing you with a service.

Every fund company wants you to invest your money with it. And each has come up with innovative products to get you started at the least possible cost.

Front-End Load

You pay a commission ranging from 2% to 9% every time you buy shares.

Back-End Load

Your entire initial investment goes into the mutual fund. You pay no direct sales commission up front. But you have to leave your money in the fund for a minimum of five or six years. Otherwise you have to pay a commission when you remove it, called a back-end load. The typical back-end-load fund charges a 6% commission in the first year, based on the value of your portfolio when you sell your shares; 5% in the second year; 4% after three years, and so on.

No-Load Funds

With no-load funds, you don't have to pay a commission to buy or sell your shares. But all mutual funds, including no-loads, pay their investment advisory team an annual management fee of between 0.2% to 2% of the fund's assets. This compensates them for making all the fund's investment decisions. Mutual funds also have to pay operating expenses to cover accounting costs, office rent, and expenses. These additional charges are deducted from the assets in the fund's portfolio.

No-load mutual funds do not provide the same quality of service as you'll receive from a professional financial planner or stockbroker. For instance, no-load fund companies will not tell you when to switch your money out of one fund that's under-performing the market and into another that's outperforming the market. Nor will they recommend a competitor's fund, no matter how well it's performing.

Beginning or busy investors should think seriously about purchasing no-load funds only through an independent financial planner or stockbroker, rather than buying the shares directly from the fund company.

Even if you have to pay a 5% to 9% commission, the potential gains of a good mutual fund over 5 to 10 years will make the commission pale by comparison.

TYPES OF FUNDS

All mutual fund families offer investors a number of different types of mutual funds from which to choose. These include:

- Equity funds
- Specialty funds
- International funds
- Bond funds
- Income funds
- Balanced funds
- Money market funds

Ideally you should diversify your investments over a number of funds. The way you diversify your portfolio will depend on the factors you considered in developing your personal financial plan.

You can find more information about each type of fund from fund dealers, banks, and financial planners.

INVESTING IN A FUND

You can invest in a mutual fund directly. Or you can work with a financial planner.

A financial planner will help you to match your needs and goals to the appropriate fund.

If you go it alone, you should call a number of fund companies—the more the better—and ask each of them for a prospectus, a booklet full of figures and tables that will tell you how and where the fund invests its money, and with what success. You should feel comfortable with the fund's past performance, future outlook, fees, rules, and regulations before you commit any money.

Since you're making your own decisions, you will deal directly with the fund company or with a discount broker.

Discount brokers charge less than a full-service broker to perform the same tasks. But they don't offer advice, and they don't really care if you make investments appropriate to your situation.

You might also consider setting up an automatic investment plan. That way, your money will be withdrawn automatically from your bank account each month and transferred directly into the mutual fund of your choice. By investing at regular intervals, you can take advantage of dollar cost averaging. By making regular investments over a sustained period, you minimize the effect of minor fluctuations in mutual fund unit costs, which can reduce the average cost of your investment.

You should also make sure all dividends and capital gains are reinvested in the fund. This will put as much money as possible to work for you in the fund.

TAX IMPLICATIONS OF MUTUAL FUNDS

Income from different mutual funds is taxed differently, depending on the type of investments the fund holds. Capital gains, for example, incur tax at a different rate than dividends. You should consider the tax implications before you invest in a mutual fund.

PRINCIPAL RESIDENCE

Your principal residence is the only asset which can grow and be sold without attracting income tax. While most individuals view their residence as their home and do not expect to sell it, it still remains a very important part of most portfolios. By paying off any mortagages quickly on your principal residence you will have an asset with which you can borrow money for other investments. The interest on this money borrowed for other income-earning investments is tax deductible. Your principal residence will increase in value over time and provide some cushion against inflation.

the business plan: cash flow is crucial

5

A business plan can serve many purposes. You can use it to guide yourself through the process of organizing and initiating your strategy. You can refer to it as your business evolves to keep yourself on track. You can use it as a road map, a reference guide, or a framework for assessing your situation and measuring your progress. If you write a business plan and never look at it again, you can use it as a doorjamb.

Writing a business plan can contribute to your confidence in the business's potential success. By considering all the elements of the business as they appear in the pages of your plan, you gain a sense of order and purpose that you may not acquire if you keep all your ideas in your head.

U.S. consultant and author David E. Gumpert advises using your business plan as a selling tool, a document "designed to convey, and support, your sense of excitement about the company. Too many business plans," he writes, "are rambling, dry, and technical, because the entrepreneurs see them as some sort of formal academic exercise."

Unlike other sales material, a business plan sells the entire company as a package. Backed by supporting evidence in the form of solid research and experience, "the business plan should convey to readers the excitement and promise that you feel."

A MIRROR TO YOUR BUSINESS SOUL

A business plan is more than a chore that you have to perform before you can pass into the inner sanctum of the entrepreneurial order. It reflects your objectives, your motives, and the philosophy behind your decision to start a business.

WHY START A BUSINESS?

Every year more than 300,000 Canadians consider starting a business. They all have their own reasons, but here are a few that some of them have in common.

1. Ego gratification: Your business will reflect your own personality and values. It will be an extension of you.

2. Challenge: You feel bored and disillusioned with all the other options for making a living, and you think you have what it takes to create something from nothing.

3. Independence: The triumphs of starting a business from scratch will be yours; so will the mistakes.

4. Legacy for the future: If you can build your idea into a thriving enterprise, you'll have something to pass on to your children when you head for the Big Business in the Sky.

5. Opportunity to make money: Experts say that money alone doesn't motivate an entrepreneur. But if there's no reward, why take the risk?

DO IT FOR OTHERS

Other people besides yourself will eventually read the document. Many of the terms and descriptions you include in the plan will already be familiar to them. They'll understand marketing strategies and financial objectives, job descriptions and legal requirements. But they will have little knowledge of the elements that make your business different from any other. These elements extend far beyond the conventional yardsticks such as sales potential and annual growth. They reflect your idiosyncracies, your likes and dislikes, your hopes and ambitions. In short, they reflect your personality.

Just as your personal financial aspirations influence your approach to running your business, your personal aspirations will influence the way you describe your business to others. As Gumpert points out, there are at least eight important reasons for writing a business plan, including:

1. To sell yourself on the business: You need to convince yourself that starting the business is right for you, from a personal and an investment viewpoint.

2. To obtain bank financing: Getting bank money is tougher than it's ever been, and a business plan is an essential component of any campaign to sell banks on your company.

3. To obtain investment funds: Venture capitalists and informal investors will ask to see your business plan. You'll also need a plan if you issue shares either privately or publicly.

4. To arrange a strategic alliance: Strategic alliances may involve joint research, marketing, development, or other cooperative endeavours between small and large companies. To persuade a corporation to work with you, you'll need a business plan.

5. To obtain large contracts: To convince a large organization to do business with you, a business plan can help. Corporations want to rely on a supplier over a period of years, not days or months. A business plan shows that you've thought about the future.

6. To attract key employees: Even in tight economies, good employees can always find work. Why should they choose your company over another, possibly larger and more prosperous? How do they know your company will even exist in another year? A written business plan can provide reassurance. A business plan also reflects your company's culture and its rationale for doing business.

7. To complete mergers and acquisitions: If you're looking for a coporate suitor to buy your business, a business plan will help. It shows the potential acquisitor that you've thought about the future and know where the business is headed. A business plan can also persuade the seller of a business that your company would make a good partner.

8. To motivate and focus your management team: In a complex organization, a business plan can help to keep everyone focused on the same goals.

BEFORE YOU TAKE THE PLUNGE

Professors at the Harvard Business School have devised 29 questions to ask yourself before you take the plunge into a new business. As you develop your business plan, you should address these questions. They'll help you to create a more comprehensive portrait of your goals and objectives.

1. How big is the window of opportunity? The conditions that lend promise to your idea for a new business will last for a specific period before they change or disappear.

2. Does the business have the potential to reward me sufficiently for my time and effort? In other words, will you get enough in return for all your time, money, sleepless nights, and marital disasters?

3. Once I've started this business, will I have further opportunities to build or add to it? You can collect golf balls every day for the rest of your life; or you can build a chain of golf courses.

4. Can the business meet unexpected obstacles and remain profitable? Your business has to make a profit through thick and thin, so make sure you don't leave yourself vulnerable to the loss of a key employee, for example, or the demise of a good customer.

5. Does anyone really need my product or service? You might think those leather hats with the feathers are just the ticket, but does anyone else?

ANXIETY RELIEF

There is a way around the inevitable anxieties that come up when you are faced with such a seemingly overwhelming task. My approach involves two facets:

1. Posing the right questions or subjects
2. Providing the bite-size answers to these questions

It is a lot easier to write a few paragraphs or even a few pages in answer to specific questions or requests than to begin writing in the abstract. The questions need not be completely answered all at once. Jot down some notes about things that occur to you immediately and think further about other matters that the question suggests. Even in answering focused questions, you often gain insights into additional research you need to do.

David Gumpert,
Creating a Successful Business Plan

6. How easily can a competitor start a similar business? The costs or the proprietary nature of your product or service may discourage others from competing against you.

7. Can I identify my customers, and will they choose to do business with me? You've probably said something to yourself like this: "There are 15 million women in Canada. All I have to do is reach 1% of them and I'll have it made." But if you can't identify the individuals who constitute that 1%—your specific customers—and persuade them to buy your product or service, your success is all in your head.

8. How much control over critical resources will my suppliers enjoy? Don't let one supplier dominate your business.

9. Will my customers be strong enough to make unreasonable demands? If General Motors tells you that it wants 10,000 of your electric motors at a price that's less than your cost of making the things, you won't have many options for survival.

10. Have I identified the skills, resources, and relationships of my business team? Ideally, the whole is greater than the sum of its parts.

11. If I haven't got it, where will I get it? Your business may not need a full-time lawyer, accountant, marketing specialist, computer technician, or other professional, but you should know where to go when you need their services.

12. What employees and equipment can my business not do without? You can make it or buy it, hire her or commission her, but you should know the advantages of each option and why they make sense for your business.

13. How much or how many do I need? If you're under-staffed, under-financed or under-stocked, you'll soon be under water.

14. What makes my business different from any other? It might be your own unique abilities; it might be the technology involved; or it might be the way you deliver your service to your customers. Whatever it is, make sure you can identify and sustain the attributes that distinguish your business from your competitors'.

15. Where can I cut corners without jeopardizing the quality of my product or service? You may not need a physicist with a Ph.D. to run your equipment, and you may not need a brand new computer for your office. You may get the same results with a technical school graduate and a used PC.

16. Have I complied with all the regulations? Your business may simply need a licence, or you may need certification from an industry standards board. Make sure you know what you need and how to meet the requirements.

17. When will I know I'm over one hurdle and moving toward the next? You have

short-term goals, like surviving until tomorrow; you have long-term goals, like generating annual revenues of $10 million in the next 10 years. Along the way, you should have mid-term checkpoints that will help you to reevaluate your strategy, realign your resources, and turn your attention to other areas of your business. Most entrepreneurs do this at regular intervals, be it monthly or quarterly.

18. Do I have enough money, talent, and time to deal with unexpected disasters? As the saying goes, a financial institution will gladly offer you an umbrella until it starts to rain. Don't wait until your business meets an unanticipated obstacle before you accumulate the resources to overcome it.

19. How can I feel confident that I have the resources I need, when I need them? You can buy a plant, hire an employee, purchase your equipment, and sign a long-term deal with your suppliers. Or you can rent space, hire employees on contract, lease your machinery, and phone your suppliers when you need them. You should know why one option makes more sense than another.

20. What are the critical motivations of potential providers of required resources and skills? People don't perform just because you pay them a lot of money. Some people want prestige; others want to avoid risk. If you know what makes your employees and suppliers tick, you can stimulate them to give you their best.

21. Can incentives be structured to meet these motivations? One employee might enjoy golfing in Hawaii; another might prefer knitting socks. A third might prefer cold hard cash. Can you provide incentives to all these employees?

22. Will my new business reward me sufficiently and allow me to meet the needs of my suppliers and employees? This refers to more than money. You may value the increased prestige that comes from running a business; your reward may lie in the lock you hold on your market or the joy of seeing your former spouse squirm at your success. Whatever it is, there has to be enough to go around.

23. How will I attract the right employees? You can hire young, raw recruits and train them; or you can hire veterans of your industry in the expectation that they will step in immediately to apply their skills. In general, though, you shouldn't hire members of your family until the business is big enough to accommodate both them and the inevitable conflicts that will arise.

24. How will my role change as the business evolves? Sooner or later, you'll have to delegate responsibility. Instead of starting a venture, you'll be managing it. You may choose to stay involved, or you may rely on professional managers to do the job for you while you think of new challenges to conquer.

25. How will I get my money out of the business? Your business may provide you with nothing more than a steady income. Or you may reap your reward by selling the company or selling stock to the public or your employees. You should understand clearly the nature of the financial rewards that you can expect to gain from your business.

26. Have I made adequate legal and financial plans for getting my money out of the business? It's not always easy to plan for the tax, legal, and financial implications of a stock offering or merger, but the better your planning the greater your potential rewards.

27. When should I cash in my chips? Maybe you need more money; maybe you foresee a decline in your market; maybe you just want to retire and play golf. The timing of the sale of your business will depend on your reasons for selling. Planning ahead allows you to determine the timing, so you can make more money.

28. Under what circumstances should I cash in my chips? Sometimes you stand to lose more than you'll gain by selling your company or taking it public. If your business is going through a rough period, you may not attract a sufficiently high price. Or you may not want to divulge proprietary information to a potential purchaser. This decision is best made with the help of sound professional advice.

29. Have I made sure that everyone will remain relatively happy when I cash in my chips? What goes around, comes around. If you don't reward your employees, partners, investors, and creditors sufficiently when you gather your rewards from your business, they probably won't do business with you again.

WHAT IF YOU DON'T HAVE A PLAN?

Lots of companies have started, grown, and prospered without a formal business plan. These include Federal Express, Nike, and Hewlett-Packard.

You're in good company if you don't have a plan. But we still don't recommend doing without one.

THE SUMMARY PLAN

Instead of preparing an exhaustive and detailed business plan, you might consider first preparing a summary. You can use this document when you apply for a bank loan, for example, since the bank will ask you for its own required details about the business, as well as personal financial information, asset valuations, and other data.

Other investors such as venture capitalists prefer to read summaries before they proceed to the next stage of their due diligence process.

WHAT SHOULD MY BUSINESS PLAN INCLUDE?

You'll need to include at least three critical pieces of information in your business plan.

1. Cash-flow projections: This will indicate how much money you can reasonably generate from your business in a specific period, such as a month or a year. Preferably you should chart two years of cash flow projections with the first four months being prepared on a weekly basis and the remaining projections on a month-to-month basis.

2. Information that your plan's readers want to know: This sounds pretty elementary, but just wait until someone who has money to invest in your business starts asking questions. You'll soon realize that you might have provided all the information that you think makes your business interesting, but little information to convince an investor that your business will provide her with a reasonable expectation of profit on her investment. In other words, provide the information that investors need rather than the information that you want them to hear. And don't assume investors know anything except how to make money.

3. How you plan to get from A to B: If your plan says you will generate revenues of $1 million in your first year, you have to show your reader how you expect to do that. How will you apply your financial backing to the nuts and bolts of your business, such as your marketing department, your support staff, your production team, and your sales staff, and how will they all work together to meet the needs of your customer and help the business reach its goals?

WHAT SHOULD MY PLAN NOT INCLUDE?

Your plan should include enough information to confirm to yourself and others that you know what you're doing and how to do it. It should not cover every possible eventuality. With this in mind, your plan should:

*   Not be too detailed. A dozen pages is sufficient; 25 pages is the maximum.
*   Be written by you, with help, perhaps, from a couple of your critical advisers, not by an outside professional planner.

• Be written in plain English, without jargon and without reference to vague or unidentified sources of income, support, or financing. Use active verbs, words of one syllable, and simple, declarative sentences.

TAKE YOUR TIME

Be prepared to devote up to 300 hours to your business plan. (That's two months, for anyone without a degree in math.) After all, you're trying to persuade an investor to put money into a venture that only you can fully understand. It probably took the investor a lot more than 300 hours to earn the money that you want him to risk.

THE PLAN

Here's the outline of a basic plan:

1. Executive Summary
   a. The business concept and the business
   b. The opportunity and strategy
   c. The target market and projections
   d. The competitive advantage
   e. The economics, profitability, and harvest potential
   f. The team
   g. The offering

2. The industry, the company and its products or services
   a. The industry
   b. The company and concept
   c. The products or services
   d. Entry and growth strategy

3. Market research and analysis
   a. Customers
   b. Market size and trends
   c. Competition and competitive edges
   d. Estimated market share and sales
   e. Ongoing market evaluation

4. The economics of the business
   a. Gross and operating margins
   b. Profit potential and durability
   c. Fixed, variable, and semivariable costs
   d. Months to break even
   e. Months to reach positive cash flow

5. Marketing plan
   a. Overall marketing strategy
   b. Pricing
   c. Sales tactics
   d. Service and warranty policies
   e. Advertising and promotion
   f. Distribution

6. Design and development plans
   a. Development status and tasks
   b. Difficulties and risks
   c. Product improvement and new products
   d. Costs
   e. Proprietary issues

7. Manufacturing and operations plan
   a. Operating cycle
   b. Geographic location
   c. Facilities and improvements
   d. Strategy and plans
   e. Regulatory and legal issues

8. Management team
   a. Organization
   b. Key management personnel
   c. Management compensation and ownership
   d. Other investors
   e. Employment and other agreements and stock option and bonus plans
   f. Board of directors

g. Other shareholders, rights and restrictions

h. Supporting professional advisers and services

9. Overall schedule

10. Critical risks, problems, and assumptions

11. The financial plan

a. Actual income statements and balance sheets

b. Pro forma income statements

c. Pro forma balance sheets

d. Pro forma cash flow analysis

e. Break-even chart and calculation

f. Cost control

g. Highlights

12. Proposed company offering

a. Desired financing

b. Offering

c. Capitalization

d. Use of funds

e. Investor's return

13. Proposed harvesting

a. How will investors get their money out?

14. Appendices

PEOPLE COME FIRST

One of the best pieces of advice about a business plan comes from William Sahlman. In describing his formula for writing a successful business plan, Sahlman cautions against focusing on numbers and forecasts without describing the people who will put the plan into action. "The plan of course should discuss specific critical numbers," he says, "such as break-even analysis, for example: the level of sales at which the business makes a profit; when does cash flow turn positive, etc."

But the important information deals with the people and the advisers upon whom the plan's success depends. "Most intelligent investors focus their attention on the people," he says. What do they know, whom do they know, how well are they known? "Investors value managers who have been around the block a few times."

The plan should describe each team member's knowledge and experience and whether the members have worked together before. It should answer such questions as:

- Where are they from?
- Where have they been educated?
- Where have they worked—and for whom?
- What have they accomplished—professionally and personally—in the past?
- What is their reputation within the business community?
- What experience do they have that's directly relevant to the opportunity they're pursuing?
- What skills, abilities, and knowledge do they have?
- How realistic are they about the venture's chances for success and the tribulations it will face?
- Who else should be on the team?
- Will they recruit high-quality people?
- How will they respond to adversity?
- Do they have the character to make the inevitable hard choices that have to be made?
- How committed are they to this venture? The size of your own investment as the business's founder speaks volumes.
- What are their motivations?

"Good people will revise their plan if necessary," Sahlman says. "But a good plan can't replace the contribution made by people."

THE BASICS OF THE FINANCIAL PICTURE
In developing your business plan, you'll have to include some figures based on a few basic calculations. These include:

- Projected expenses
- Projected income statement
- Cash flow
- Balance sheet
- Current and quick ratios

EXPENSES

Initial one-time expenses incurred in starting your business might include:

- Rent deposit or down payment on property
- Fixtures and equipment
- Vehicles
- Start-up inventory
- Renovation of premises
- Licences and permits
- Installation of equipment
- Legal costs

Once you've estimated these costs, you should add about another 50% to the total amount to cover unexpected costs, which cover everything from delays in constructuion to equipment repairs.

Day-to-day operating expenses include:

- Wages and salaries, including your own
- Rent or mortgage payments
- Raw materials
- Telephone
- Utilities
- Distribution
- Insurance
- Advertising and promotion
- Stationery and office supplies
- Legal and accounting fees
- Maintenance
- Sales expenses
- Transportation and travel
- Debt repayment

- Bad debts, discounts, and so on
- Other expenses, including depreciation

THE INCOME STATEMENT

In the income statement, you can forecast your company's revenues for the first year on a monthly or weekly basis, including any seasonal or monthly variations. The income statement will also include the cost of producing a product or service to meet anticipated sales projections, including fixed and variable expenses. Based on these figures, you can determine your projected pretax net profit or loss.

From this figure, you subtract a provision for taxes. This gives you your net income.

THE CASH-FLOW FORECAST

The essence of your company's survival lies in its cash flow. Companies live or die by their cash flow. You can actually run out of cash and go broke even as you make a major sale that will provide your business with a profit.

You may sell like there's no tomorrow, and you may anticipate revenues that will keep you in clover for years. You may also forget that tomorrow you have to pay your income tax installment or pay off your equipment loan. And you may forget that the company that accounts for one-third of your sales also takes six months to pay its bills.

Unless you know how much money is actually flowing in and out of your company from day to day, week to week, and month to month, and how much money you actually have in your hand, all the sales and revenue statements in the world will do you no good. Without a firm grasp of your company's cash flow, you can't make effective decisions about spending, borrowing, or expanding your business. By monitoring cash flow on a regular basis as cash comes in and goes out, you can record the pulse of your company's lifeblood so you can plan into the future. You'll appreciate these figures if you want to expand or tackle new markets. With a cash-flow forecast, you can determine the effect of such actions on the flow of cash and determine whether you'll need outside financing or whether you can support the expanded business from funds generated internally.

With a cash-flow projection, you can estimate income and outflow month by month. To prepare a cash-flow projection, consider:

- Your ratio of cash sales to credit sales
- Terms of your sales (e.g., net 10 days)
- How promptly you must pay suppliers
- How often you pay employees and consultants
- Interest and principal payments and their frequency on any loans
- Inventory required to meet projected sales
- Planned purchases of fixed assets

You should also make sure you prepare for unexpected disruptions of your forecasts.

Cash flow is usually monitored on a monthly basis. You start with the cash on hand at the beginning of the month. You then add the receipts during the month from customer payments and any other sources. Then you subtract disbursements—your fixed and variable expenses.

This tells you the amount of cash you have available at the end of the month. Cash flow is the difference between the cash on hand at the beginning and the cash at the end for each period being measured.

THE BALANCE SHEET

With a balance sheet, you can estimate the financial condition of your business at the end of the next six or twelve months or even further ahead in the future. It lists current assets, such as accounts receivable, the value of inventory, and cash available. It also lists the value of fixed assets such as property, equipment, fixtures, and vehicles, after depreciation.

Current liabilities listed in a balance sheet might include any bills due within a year. Long-term liabilities include loans with a term of more than a year, such as mortgages, equipment loans, and loans that you or others have made to your business.

WORKING CAPITAL

By calculating the difference between your company's current assets and current liabilities, you can determine its working capital. This is the amount of money you can use to invest in expansion, new equipment, product development, or other initiatives.

POSSIBLY UNBALANCED

The balance sheet is often more important for manufacturing companies than for service companies, which usually don't have many hard assets like machinery and real estate. In fact, a service organization's balance sheet can be misleading, since its primary assets are its people, whose value is difficult to measure in a balance sheet.

BUSINESS RATIOS

These will help you to measure the performance of your business and compare it to others in your industry. Each industry adheres to different ratios, so you should talk to your accountant about the ones that apply to yours. If these ratios change unexpectedly, you should examine your calculations or figure out where the problem lies in your business.

The current ratio is equivalent to your current assets divided by your current liabilities. If your assets exceed your liabilities by a ratio of two to one (2:1), then your business is probably in good shape; if your liabilities exceed your assets by two to one, you might have trouble meeting your debts. The ideal ratio for your business depends on your company's cash flow and other factors.

The quick ratio is calculated by subtracting inventory from assets and dividing the figure by current liabilities. A ratio of 1:1 is good, but the ideal figure depends on your industry. The quick ratio indicates the ease with which your company could sell its liquid assets to raise money to meet its debts.

LOOKING FOR A STRATEGIC PARTNER

As an alternative to expansion, a small company may look for a corporate partner to share opportunities and resources. Major corporations look at a number of factors before committing themselves to a small strategic partner. A detailed business plan will help you achieve your objectives, if you decide to follow this route.

THE OPERATING PLAN

As your company grows, you can use your business plan as a mechanism for keeping your management team focused on the same goals.

"For the business plan to be effective in keeping everyone on track though, it must contain a level of detail not necessary in either a summary or full plan," says David Gumpert. "An operational plan must get into the details of distribution, production, and other areas that are essential to making certain everyone understands what is expected. Indeed managers often welcome such detail so they know clearly what they need to work toward."

You can use your basic business plan to take the steps necessary to start your business: raising money, hiring employees, negotiating with suppliers and customers, and keeping the business on track. As your business grows, you can revise and augment your business plan, with contributions from your key employees, and use the document as a planning tool for future growth.

financing your
business

Entrepreneurs have to think about raising money as a dynamic function. The process continues throughout all stages of the business. Managing and raising cash is probably the most important aspect of running a small company—along with all the other functions that can make or break the business. The entrepreneur has to constantly develop and revise strategies and analyses to figure out how much the business needs and when it will need it.

6

Almost by definition, starting and building a business places severe constraints on your personal and business financial resources. Your prime financial concern, at least initially, will be to maintain sufficient liquidity to reach your objectives. You'll be working under intense conditions: situations will arise every day that will require your full attention. At the same time as you address these issues, you also have to assess the financial health of your business constantly.

In the early stages of growth, a business doesn't generate enough cash to pay for sophisticated advisory services or to hire and train specialized employees. Entrepreneurs themselves may be skilled in a particular area of business, but may be only vaguely familiar with the specifics of finance, accounting, or administration. As they chart their way through unfamiliar territory, with their very survival at stake, most entrepreneurs can't afford to take radical steps to build their organizations. Instead, they're better advised to take one small but important step at a time.

Because of the number and urgency of the problems that confront a new business, and because of the limitations on your own resources, you'll likely follow a conservative growth strategy. In fact, small companies seem to do best with conservative growth strategies. You'll also feel more confident about the future of your business if you stick to the basics. (That's why a business plan helps. It reminds you of the basic assumptions and tools that you defined before you started to build your organization.)

PERSONAL SURVIVAL COMES FIRST

It may take several years before your company starts to generate enough money to provide you with an income. In the meantime, you have to survive. From the outset, you should have the mechanisms in place to give you access to the money you need to live. A line of credit or an overdraft, for example, will come in handy when you face an emergency.

GROWTH VERSUS SURVIVAL

If you enjoy the perks of running your own company but still want to find time to spend with your family, taking weekends off at home and summers at the cottage, you probably don't want to grow your business rapidly, if at all. It takes time, energy, and money to build a business. All three of these factors have serious implications for your personal life.

As we've discussed earlier, many entrepreneurs enjoy the sense of autonomy they derive from running their own operation. They make the decisions, they make the mistakes, and they take the credit for their success. At the end of the day, they close the door and go home, satisfied that they've put their time, energy, and money to its best possible use, but satisfied, as well, that they've achieved a balance between their business and personal lives that satisfies their needs.

If you decide that you want to dedicate yourself to growing your business, however, you can follow several steps. Many of these steps have been tested and proven by other fast-growing organizations, from Intuit software to Callaway golf clubs. Like starting a business, growing one requires focus, dedication, perseverance, and financial resources. The better organized you are at the outset, the better your chances of success.

TIPS FOR SUCCESSFUL GROWTH

Here's a summary of the factors that have contributed to the expansion of numerous successful companies:

- Careful planning, from the outset, with a detailed business plan
- Prior experience with start-up business by founder or a member of the team
- Research into competition, customers, market, and so on
- Defined target, realistic ambitions
- Product or service that satisfies customer expectations
- Prior experience in targetted industry
- Appropriate level of technology
- Focus on customer satisfaction
- Emphasis on high-quality product or service
- Solicitation of customer views
- Simplicity
- Awareness of change, appropriate responses
- Appropriate use of professional advisers
- Well-considered growth strategy; no impulsive moves

Source: The Entrepreneur's Complete Sourcebook

EXPANDING YOUR BUSINESS

By taking a methodical and prudent approach to expanding your business, you can avoid mistakes and take full advantage of opportunities as they arise. Expansion can involve several different strategies, including:

- Expansion of physical geographic market
- Expansion of capacity
- Expansion of product or service lines
- Merger or acquisition

- Franchising
- Revised strategic objectives

Expansion may not be a simple option for your business; it may be a necessity. In some industries, businesses don't survive unless they expand. To remain competitive, these businesses have to grow.

Expansion brings other advantages, however, beyond survival. For the founder, it brings the satisfaction and power of running a larger enterprise. Expansion should increase revenues, and it may also increase profits (although profits won't increase automatically). A larger company may give you an advantage over your competitors, and the winning attitude that comes with expansion may energize and motivate your team.

Expansion doesn't come without a cost, however. After all your efforts to expand your business, you may find your profits haven't grown at all and might even have diminished. Expansion also consumes resources in the form of employee time, management expertise, and financing. In the process of expanding, you may lose your focus on your primary objectives, giving your competitors an opportunity to entice customers away from your company. In the process of expanding, you may also enter unfamiliar markets, which may even bring you into competition with current customers or suppliers.

Careful planning can address many of these disadvantages. But you'll still need sufficient resources to expand your business without mishap.

To minimize the problems and ensure that your expansion proceeds as smoothly as possible, you should reevaluate your business plan and marketing plan in light of your current objectives. Using some of the procedures we'll explore later in this chapter, you should also evaluate your finances to make sure you have the resources required to expand steadily. If you don't, you should plan your strategy for accumulating these resources. By surveying your customers, you can determine how your expansion will affect your ability to deliver what they need, when they need it. You should also consult your advisers to get their opinions about your organization's strengths and weaknesses and its ability to withstand the pressures of expansion.

What You Need to Know to Determine How Much You Need

As we've discussed throughout the first chapters of this book, entrepreneurs take a much different approach to planning, starting, building, and financing their organizations from big companies. These differences extend to the way in which entrepreneurs manage their organizations and the way in which they use the financial tools common to small and big organizations. In managing their financial affairs, entrepreneurs apply different principles from larger organizations. These principles become apparent in determining such critical variables as cash flow, the break-even point, return on investment, and debt-equity ratio.

Smaller companies not only generate lower sales with fewer assets and fewer employees than big companies, they also have far fewer financial resources to support them in their operations and growth. U.S. entrepreneurs and consultants John A. Welsh and Jerry F. White call this condition "resource poverty." According to these experts, resource poverty requires a much different approach to management from the entrepreneur.

Resource poverty, the authors say, arises from a number of conditions. Small companies tend to operate in highly fragmented industries such as wholesaling, retailing, services, and job-shop manufacturing. To build revenues and gain a competitive advantage, these companies resort primarily to price cutting. But excessive price cutting quickly eliminates profits and deprives the business of a critical source of financing for expansion.

In such a context, entrepreneurs have to decide whether they can afford to defer the financial rewards they seek in return for starting and running a business. As we've mentioned, if entrepreneurs pay themselves a salary, this expense usually represents a much larger percentage of a company's revenues than executive salaries in a bigger company, often such a large fraction, say Welsh and White, that little is left to pay additional managers, to reward investors, or to finance expansion. Nor can small companies use their own financial resources to pay for the specialized accounting and bookkeeping services they need to expand steadily or to test and train new employees in advance.

Operating under such severe constraints on their resources, small companies are much more susceptible to mistakes or mismanagement. They're also more seriously affected by external forces such as changes in regulations and rising interest rates.

That's the bad news. The good news is that small companies have some advantages over their larger competitors. They're more flexible, for example, and more responsive to change. They can seize opportunities more quickly as long as they have the resources to act at the opportune moment. To make the best use of their limited resources, White and Welsh advise small companies to apply some special financial management tools.

CASH-FLOW FORECASTING

The investment required to finance growth comes either from a company's internally generated resources or from outside investors and lenders. In planning for profitable growth, however, entrepreneurs often underestimate the volatility in patterns of cash flowing in and out of their organizations. This volatility undermines their ability to plan for profitable operation, let along for expansion. Over the course of a year, the entrepreneur will likely have to convince her bank manager that the business can survive, even though she knows that the company has the resources not only to survive but to expand.

In a big business, as Welsh and White observe, cash flow equals net profit plus depreciation and amortization. The system is in perfect equilibrium, and small distortions caused by delayed payments or mismatched purchases don't significantly distort the underlying principle. A big company also has the financial capacity to borrow short-term funds to meet any requirements caused by minor fluctuations.

A small and growing company doesn't enjoy such resources. By following the conventional approach to cash-flow forecasting, small companies often find themselves consistently strapped for the cash required simply to stay in business. With lenders and investors scrutinizing the organization's finances, the company has little or no room for expansion.

In a small company, cash on hand fluctuates wildly: Suppliers demand payment while customers delay payments. Over the long term, a small company may record excellent performance. Its customers may be highly creditworthy and reliable. But lenders remain skeptical if receivables don't balance with inventories and if debt doesn't correspond properly to assets revenues, and equity. Even if the entrepreneur knows the distortions are temporary, the small company has no track record to reassure lenders. At some point, the entrepreneur will certainly have to provide a personal guarantee for short-term financing against either receivables or equipment. Under such conditions, who can think of expansion?

The Cash Factors

Consider this small company: Its expenses include taxes, labour costs, materials, and marketing services. The company pays for these products and services promptly. New equipment is depreciated steadily, month by month. Meanwhile, customers usually pay predictably within 45 days of month-end. Increased sales, on paper at least, lead directly to increased profits.

Unfortunately, profits on paper don't always correspond to profits in cold hard cash. Many of the small company's financial resources are consumed or accounted for by unshipped products, future contracts, accounts receivable, and materials purchased in advance to meet future requirements. Even when the entrepreneur coordinates the writing of cheques with the receipt of payments and collects promptly on accounts when they come due, cash flow remains out of whack. "The problem," observe Welsh and White, "is that not all of the cash has flowed yet. When the boxes and the little pieces of paper are converted to cash, it will flow."

In such a situation, a small company depends as much on credit lines extended by suppliers and its providers of general and administratvie services as on its own resources. In fact, as sales and profits rise, on paper, cash flow actually declines.

Coping With Cash Flow

In a small company, cash often arrives long after the company has invested its financial resources in manufacturing the product or developing the service required to earn it. These variations in sales create periods of rapid growth and contraction. During one period, the company may consume cash to finance production, while, during the next period, when the company has no immediate production requirements, cash flows in, creating a surplus. The entrepreneur has to recognize this cash for what it is: money to cover past expenses and future growth. It is not the entrepreneur's personal reward for a job well done. "All too often, however," say Welsh and White, "a new car or a vacation trip consumes this war chest, which will be sorely needed for the next period of high sales."

To repond to large and severe short-term fluctuations in a growing business, an entrepreneur must focus initially on the way cash flows into and out of the company. One of the most understandable ways to monitor cash needs and cash availability is to show the future operations of the business through a simultaneous portrayal of the income statement and the statement of receipts and disbursements over successive short periods, covering the next six months or one year. The entrepreneur can then update this forecast at least monthly.

The many different cycles of payments will account for the noticeable differences between cash and profit over each short period. The entrepreneur may pay salaries and wages, for example, on a weekly, biweekly, monthly, and semimonthly basis. The company may pay its taxes on a monthly or quarterly basis. Only a few expenses will actually conform to the uniform monthly cycle portrayed by the income statement.

For the entrepreneur, who must worry about this week's payroll, profit is not cash, and profit plus depreciation is not the available cash flow. By forecasting and comparing net income, receipts, and expenditures over a specified short period, however, the entrepreneur can address the problems created by the volatility in the flow of cash through the business.

BREAKING EVEN

To determine the revenues required to finance a new business, a new product, market expansion, or increased production capacity, conventional wisdom requires a break-even analysis. This analysis is based on some simple concepts: Sales rise in proportion to units ordered, produced, and shipped or services provided. Expenses can be defined as fixed and variable.

Fixed expenses such as mortgage payments must be met whether or not sales are made. The organization pays variable expenses such as labour, materials, and marketing costs in almost direct proportion to the units shipped. Total expenses equal the sum of the fixed and variable expenses.

In plotting a conventional break-even analysis, dollars are represented on a vertical axis and units shipped per month are represented on the horizontal axis. Over the period, two straight lines rise to the right, intersecting at the point where the number of units shipped per period will make revenue equal to expenses.

Unfortunately for start-up companies, break-even points remain infuriatingly elusive. This can have serious consequences. By underestimating your break-even point, you may plan confidently for the moment when you can take the first step in your expansion plans, only to find that, instead of breaking even, your company has actually lost money. In the meantime, by operating on a shoestring and paying yourself little or no salary, you stretch your business and personal resources to the limit, only to find that you require more money, more time, and more effort just to break even.

What's the problem? The answer can lie in several areas of your operation. First, you can underestimate fixed expenses. Although a conventional break-even analysis shows sales and expenses growing almost in direct proportion, conventional analysis may not take into account such elements as discounts for volume sales, bonuses, and free samples. For small companies in the initial stages of existence, expenses rise not in a straight line but in stages, depending on the approach taken to generate additional sales, producing a series of break-even points.

During the initial stages, a company may operate to the full capacity of its resources and facilities. Direct expenses can be calculated fairly predictably per unit of production. But incidental expenses associated with growth, such as warehousing, materials handling, and marketing costs may create serious distortions between the company's projected and actual break-even point.

Nor do entrepreneurs have access to the expertise required to analyze and define these incidental expenses and their projected impact on the business. By definition, the new company has little past history to use in predicting indirect expenses. Instead, entrepreneurs have to rely for their decisions on intuition, necessity, or ambition.

An entrepreneur needs detailed and conservative planning tools to create an accurate break-even analysis. Otherwise, mistakes made at this stage of a business can threaten or destroy the operation. By using generalities and broad assumptions to calculate a company's break-even point, an entrepreneur can develop false expectations.

The more detailed the forecast of your company's future operations, the better you can plan for survival and growth. You can use your income statement, for example, to plan for a variety of possibilities, changing the details to produce various outcomes and responding accordingly.

MAXIMIZE INVESTOR RETURNS

In planning your growth strategy, for example, one of your objectives will likely be to maximize the return on your investment. After all, it's your business, and you invested your money, possibly with money from other sources, to get the business off the ground. While you might have other objectives, depending on your personal goals and values, increasing the value of your investment will most likely rank among the measures of your entrepreneurial success.

As we'll see in the following pages, however, this measurement may take a considerable period to satisfy the expectations of the entrepreneur and other investors in the company. In the initial stages of the business, return on investment occupies a secondary position to other more important priorities, especially cash flow.

EXPANDING TO INCREASE PROFIT AND RETURN

In the company's earliest stages, the entrepreneur has to focus on making a sale and producing the required product or service. As sales and production become comfortably predictable, the entrepreneur can turn her attention to the next step: to generate a profit and cash flow. Only after profit and cash flow become steady or at least manageable can the entrepreneur devote time and energy to the next requirement: improving the efficiency with which the organization generates a profit.

Unfortunately, entrepreneurs often become obsessed with profit and cash flow, never accumulating the resources or the confidence to move to the third stage of development. As they discover, a small operation can survive for a surprisingly long period without generating a profit. Cash flow, not profit, determines survival.

Only when the company can't meet a critical payment does it encounter problems. This happens not when profits flag but when cash flow stops.

An entrepreneur's first priority is to maintain cash flow or liquidity. Some profit is necessary. But in the inital stages, at least, the efficiency with which the company generates the profit—the return on investment—is far less important than cash flow.

If the entrepreneur wants to expand the business, however, the company must first earn back its start-up losses, a process that can take a considerable amount of time. In the meantime, the company's balance sheet and debt-equity ratio will horrify potential lenders, who look at such figures in determining a company's eligibility for financing. As Welsh and White observe, "The small business that survives start-up losses may have excellent capacity to service an additional debt burden. But the business must generate sales and earnings for a considerable period before its net equity on the balance sheet approaches a reasonable sum acceptable to most bankers and investors."

Lenders and investors alike will hesitate before they put more money into a company that has exhausted its resources during the start-up phase. The balance sheet looks terrible. The company has no prolonged track record. Management is likely exhausted. And projections are nothing more than the entrepreneur's wishful thinking recorded on pieces of paper. Now investors want their money back, along with a reasonable return. The original investors may have no patience left, just when patience is the only thing they need to see their investment objectives fulfilled. In response, the entrepreneur can make only a limited number of moves.

IMPROVE EARNINGS TO IMPROVE THE DEBT-EQUITY RATIO

The most important step the entrepreneur can take is to improve the organization's debt-equity ratio. To this end, the entrepreneur has to improve earnings. You can do this by increasing sales, but as we've discussed, sales growth requires cash.

You can also increase earnings by improving your profit margin. Profit margins can be improved by reducing and limiting expenses, for example, improving productivity, or increasing prices, if your market will tolerate it.

As the owner of the business, you also can rearrange the company's liabilities to improve its debt-equity ratio. Welsh and White describe, for example, the owner/manager who borrowed $25,000 from a relative on a one-year note with an annual rollover provision. By changing the loan to a personal obligation and persuading the relative to accept common stock in payment of the company's obligation, the entrepreneur reduced the company's debt by $25,000, increasing its equity by an equal amount. The move had a dramatic effect on the organization's debt-equity ratio.

LOOKING FOR A DEAL

As we'll discuss later, once an entrepreneur gets his company's finances in order, he can start looking for capital in the form of debt or equity to expand the business further. There are a number of different sources that an entrepreneur can tap for investment or financing. Each has its own advantages and disadvantages. But as consultant William Sahlman points out, the entrepreneur should take care to make sure he gets the right financing from the right sources, even in the early stages of the business.

"From whom you raise capital is often more important than the terms," says Sahlman. "Unsophisticated investors panic in the face of disaster; they refuse to invest more and want to get their money out. Sophisticated investors roll up their sleeves and pitch in to get the company back on track. They can recruit and motivate team members."

According to Sahlman, the best deals have six characteristics:

1. They're simple.
2. They're fair.
3. They emphasize trust rather than legal ties.
4. They don't blow apart if actual differs slightly from plan.
5. They don't provide perverse incentives that inspire people to behave weirdly.
6. They're written on a pile of papers no thicker than one-quarter of an inch.

In the next chapter, we'll explore these criteria in more detail.

sources
of
finance

Once you've successfully established your company, wrestled with its finances to get its balance sheet and other indices in order, and determined how much money you need and why you need it, it is time to start looking for other sources of capital.

7

As we mentioned in the previous chapter, the source of the money can be as important as the money itself. Especially in the early stages of a business, inexperienced lenders and investors can contribute as much disruption as support to your business. Experienced investors, on the other hand, contribute far more than money.

Before you go looking for money; however, you have to figure out exactly how much you need, why you need it, for how long you'll need it, and how you'll pay it back. Investors will assess your talent, character, and forecasts in making their decision to support you. Your character, though it's intangible, will weigh heavily on their minds. But they'll also want to know what they're getting for their money, what you intend to do with it, and when they'll get it back.

Some investors will provide money to finance the acquisition of hard assets like land, buildings, and equipment. They provide long-term funding, usually in the form of a mortgage or term loan; a long-term lease; or the sale of stock.

Other investors provide working capital so you can meet your short-term financial obligations and pay your bills. Commercial lenders, for example, provide short-term loans secured by receivables or inventory; lines of credit; and other types of financing.

Before you go looking for money, you have to know why you need it and how you'll pay it back. Mismatching your sources of funding with the application of the funds can lead to problems. Likewise, the more sources of capital you consider, the more attention you'll pay to your spending and the tighter control you'll have over your company's finances.

CONSERVE YOUR RESOURCES

"If there's any way at all you can get away without spending money, don't spend it. Make sure you manage your overhead and minimize, minimize, minimize everything possible."

Kent Groves, Founder, Maritime Trading Co.

DON'T UNDERESTIMATE

As we discussed briefly in the previous chapter, entrepreneurs often underestimate the amount of money they'll need to get their new business up and running. Some may get a business up, but lack the money to get it running. Some may even get it running, but exhaust their finances before they can gather enough momentum to keep it going.

This happens for many reasons. Here are a few:

1. Knowing the value of a dollar, entrepreneurs assume they can squeeze the maximum value out of every dollar they can beg, borrow, or steal to start their businesses. They leave no room for mistakes, surprises, or unexpected challenges.

2. Entrepreneurs focus so intently on the challenge of putting their ideas into practice and marketing their product or service that they neglect the more mundane aspects of running a business, like payables, receivables, and simple accounting.

3. Acting on their own, often without a team of managers or advisers to guide them, entrepreneurs devote all their resources to a single objective, leaving nothing in reserve for unexpected obstacles or opportunities.

4. Entrepreneurs overestimate their ability to generate revenues.

PROFIT MAGAZINE'S TOP 10 FINANCING TIPS

James Dean and Grant Simons prepared this list of tips for *Profit Magazine*.

1. Understand the nature of banks and their business before you get frustrated by their inability to give you everything you want.

2. Develop a long-term financing strategy.

3. Find financing to suit your business. Some investors know more than others about your industry.

4. Use your contacts. Friends, family, and other entrepreneurs can give you good advice.

5. Consider suppliers as sources of financing. They can extend trade credit, for example, or provide lease financing of inventory.

6. Reexamine the capital structure of your business from time to time to make sure it's still appropriate. The proportion of bank financing, owner's equity, and private investment, for example, may rise or fall, depending on the circumstances.

7. Be prepared to walk away from a deal you don't like. If it's too expensive, too restrictive, or too unwieldy, the financing may not make sense for your business.

8. Consider other ways to find financing. Payments in advance, for example, can provide a cushion to get you through a production period.

9. Do you want control or do you want growth? Sometimes financing for growth comes at the cost of giving up control. Can you handle that?

10. Regard your lenders as suppliers. They need your business as much as you need their product, which in this case happens to be money.

SOURCES, FROM A TO Z

The most accessible and unconditional source of funds for your new venture is your own accumulated wealth. It's also the first source you should tap, not only because it's the most accessible, but because many people won't lend to or invest in your business if you haven't invested at least some of your own money first. You have to put your money where your mouth is to establish your credibility.

If you have a bank account, stocks or bonds, real estate, or a life insurance policy, you have something to invest in your business. You can also borrow money using some of these assets as collateral.

YOUR MONEY COMES FIRST

In starting a new business, almost 80% of entrepreneurs in Canada rely on their own savings.

SOURCE NUMBER TWO

Without going too far afield, you have access to other sources of short-term credit that you may not have considered. These include:

1. Credit cards: More than one entrepreneur has taken a cash advance against every credit card in his pocket, confident that he can pay the money back as soon as the business starts to generate some revenues. There are certainly cheaper sources of debt financing. But in the initial stages of your business, with no money coming in and lots of money flowing out, you may not qualify for a loan.

2. Trade credit: If your suppliers like you and believe in your plan to build a business, they'll often provide you with their goods or services and allow you to pay for them later. In return, they receive your loyal patronage, assuming you pay them as agreed.

3. Customers: Depending on the type of business you start, you can often work with your customers to share the costs of a project. A contractor, for example, can provide her services while the customer pays for the materials. You can also negotiate with customers to provide you with partial payments over the course of a project especially if it takes several months. Or you can ask customers to pay up front for a product or service.

4. Real estate: As we mentioned earlier, you can borrow money using your house or other property as collateral for the loan. Just make sure you talk to your spouse before you put the family home on the line.

5. Equipment: Instead of using your own money to buy a new kiln dryer, why not obtain an equipment loan, secured by the equipment itself, that you can pay back over several years? Alternatively, why not lease the equipment? You could also buy a used one, which is a lot cheaper and just as effective.

LOVE MONEY: FRIENDS AND RELATIVES

Once you've exhausted your personal resources, the next likely source of funds is friends and relatives. At least one-quarter of all entrepreneurs in Canada rely on friends and relatives for at least part of their start-up financing.

Friends and relatives know you (and presumably that's not a drawback). They'll give you a break, and they'll be more inclined than a commercial investor or lender to support you on the basis of your potential success alone.

Be prepared, however, for your friends and relatives to pay close attention to what you're doing with their money. In return for their support, they may expect a detailed lesson in business. They may also get cold feet at the first sign of trouble and ask for their money back.

If that time comes, you might have to decide which you value more: the support and love of your relatives and the comfort of your friendships, or the money that your friends and relatives provide.

To persuade a friend or relative to support your new venture, you should prepare yourself just as you would to borrow from a bank or raise capital from an investor. A business plan helps. So does all the other information that you've accumulated. You should also prepare a formal repayment schedule so that the investor knows how and when you plan to provide a return on the investment. In fact, the more formal and detailed your agreement, the fewer surprises or unpleasant conflicts you'll encounter in your dealings with friends and relatives. Operating in a businesslike way not only puts the transaction in a well-defined context, it may also salvage the relationship if anything goes wrong.

ANGEL FINANCING

Angels are individuals who enjoy the thrill, the challenge, and the satisfaction of investing in new ventures. As their name implies, angels appear from the most unlikely places and at the most unlikely times to help you start your new business. But they don't usually appear unless you spend some time looking for them.

Angels are often entrepreneurs themselves. They know how it feels to search far and wide for money, when they know full well that their idea would work if only they had the resources. But how do you find these angels?

Like heaven itself, the place where financial angels hang out has yet to be discovered. But you can reach out to them through your own network of professionals, who might have reason to deal with them and who might put in a good word for you.

These intermediaries include accountants, lawyers, bankers, consultants, and financial planners, especially ones who deal with entrepreneurs as a regular part of their business and who are familiar with you and your capabilities as a businessperson.

DEBT FINANCING: BANKS

It's easier to explain the role of banks to a start-up business by describing what they don't do. Banks don't

- Risk their depositors' money on new ventures;
- Provide equity financing to entrepreneurs without assets;
- Speculate on tomorrow's successful new business without some reassurance that the business can survive today;
- Lend money unless they're pretty sure they can get it back, on time and with interest;
- Extend a loan to you just because you've dealt with the same bank for 12 years.

The critical factor in an entrepreneur's relationship with a bank could be summarized in a single word: communication. Bankers and their clients alike share the responsibility for open communication.

Entrepreneurs have an infinite capacity to identify new opportunities. But sometimes they need to temper their unbridled optimism with a dose of reality. In many cases, the lesson in reality comes from a beleaguered banker.

FAST OUT, SLOW IN

"Most entrepreneurs who start a business run out of cash at a faster rate than they bring in customers and profitable sales."

Jeffry Timmons, Babson College

WHAT BANKS DO

Banks provide financing to qualified customers, usually in the form of a loan, and usually secured by a fixed asset like real estate or equipment. If your business has no fixed assets, the bank will ask you to use your personal assets as security. If you have no unencumbered personal assets, you may be out of luck.

Banks will also provide you with support and referrals to other services, if you need them, if you have a good relationship with your banker, and if you make it clear what you need.

Banks in Canada go out of their way to attract entrepreneurial business customers. Not only is it politically expedient to deal with such companies, but the banks make money from them, as well. Internal surveys by banks themselves have shown that entrepreneurial customers contribute more on a per capita basis than any other type of customer to the organization's bottom line. Entrepreneurs tend to combine their business and personal banking at the same institution and, as long as the relationship remains smooth, they tend to remain as customers for the long haul.

Nevertheless, when an unprepared entrepreneur walks into a bank, asks for a loan and is refused, it's easy to blame the bank for letting down the entrepreneur. When a bank calls a loan because a business has violated a condition of the loan or missed a payment or lost a major customer, it's easy for the business to say that the bank has threatened its existence; it's more difficult for the bank to say that a failed business, with annual sales of about $1 million, threatens the existence of the bank, with annual sales of $10 billion.

By the same token, banks themselves do an awful job of letting the public know how well they actually serve their entrepreneurial customers. They also do a terrible job of informing the public about the margins on which they operate.

Short-Term Financing

To qualify for short-term bank financing, your business needs to generate sufficient cash flow (not profits) to meet the payment schedule. Here are the types of financing that banks provide.

Short-Term Loan

Usually repaid within 30 to 180 days, entrepreneurs use short-term loans of $50,000 to $100,000 to cover cash-flow shortages, purchase inventory, or take advantage of supplier discounts. Often a short-term loan is secured by a personal guarantee or company assets, or extended solely on the basis of the company's financial statements, track record, and ability to repay the loan. Such loans are usually extended as demand loans. This means the bank can demand payment in part or in full whenever it wants. In practice, a bank seldom calls a demand loan unless its funds are in jeopardy. If you have a demand loan, however, you should realize that the bank can demand that you pay it back if your financial situation deteriorates or if the bank becomes uncomfortable with your financial situation.

Line of Credit

Like a short-term loan, a line of credit is a secured or unsecured facility that gives an entrepreneur quick access to credit without red tape or negotiation. The line of credit is negotiated once. When it's in place, you can use it and repay the money, with interest, at your convenience, as long as you remain within your credit limit. You qualify for a line of credit based on your income and/or assets and other personal obligations. This means that you're borrowing on your net worth—the difference between your total assets minus your total debt. With a credit line, there are usually no fixed payment schedules; you pay interest each month and repay principal on an irregular basis. Sometimes you pledge assets as security. These assets may include accounts receivable, cars, stocks, or bonds. Sometimes another person, who has a greater net worth, may co-sign for the credit line with you and assume responsibility for repaying your loan if you can't.

Receivable Financing

Banks will usually lend about 65% to 80% of the value of your approved receivables on a short-term basis. Receivables usually have to be under 90 days old, involving customers who are good credit risks. A bank would likely extend credit on a 30-day receivable with Bell Canada; a 120-day receivable with a pizza shop in a small town may not be to the bank's liking.

With all these loans, the bank has to stay informed about your business, the condition of your accounts, your sales and earnings record, and other critical data. If you don't provide this to the bank willingly and promptly on a monthly basis or even more frequently, the bank will become nervous.

Long-Term Financing

Lenders provide long-term loans for a year or more to cover the cost of major acquisitions such as land, equipment, and machinery.

Equipment Loans

Secured by the equipment itself, these loans usually cover 60% to 80% of the cost of the equipment. You repay a long-term equipment loan through cash flow, not profits. So the bank will look closely at your income statements when it evaluates your worthiness as a borrower.

Equipment Leases

Equipment leases are extended to companies that don't want to tie up their own cash in purchasing or borrowing to buy equipment. With an equipment lease, you have the use of the equipment, but the lender holds title to it. A lease can provide tax and other advantages, because the bank or leasing company legally owns your asset and charges you a monthly lease payment. At the end of the lease's term, the asset often carries a residual value, which determines the amount you'll pay to discharge the lease. You may also have the option of returning the leased equipment to the bank or leasing company.

Real Estate Loan

Extending for as long as 25 years, a real estate loan usually covers about 75% of the market value of a property, which is used to secure the loan. By making small monthly payments, the entrepreneur has the use of the property for a long period while keeping cash free to apply to other purposes. The bank can take back your property if you can't meet the payment schedule.

HOW MUCH SHOULD YOU BORROW?

There may be a difference between how much you *can* borrow and how much you *should* borrow: You may have the capacity to pay back a larger loan than you need. Or you may need more money than you can handle based on your financial situation or the security that you can provide for the loan.

Your bank determines your ability to repay a loan based on many factors including your income, net worth, and credit history. With this in mind, the bank wants to know how much you already owe, the value of your assets, your personal and business annual earnings, and your track record in repaying your loans in the past. If you have a bad record with another financial institution or a Credit Bureau, you'll have to provide solid evidence that your situation has changed or you may encounter some difficulty obtaining another loan.

The size of the loan you need depends primarily on the difference between your anticipated expenses and your anticipated income. Ideally, the loan should provide you with enough money to cover the difference.

The size of the loan for which you can qualify depends primarily on your expected cash flow. Cash flow indicates your ability to pay back the loan.

Before you approach a bank for a loan, you should have at your fingertips all the information that a bank or your investors would require, including your financial history, your credit history, your current financial circumstances, your business plan, and your résumé.

THE SEVEN CS OF CREDIT FINANCING

About half of all entrepreneurs in Canada approach a bank for debt financing. If you're one of them, you can prepare yourself for the exercise by considering the criteria that account managers use in evaluating your application. They're sometimes called the seven Cs of credit.

1. Character: Your personal credit history reveals volumes about your character. It shows whether you've paid attention to your own finances in the past, repaying loans, for example, and keeping control of your other debts. Your credit history will also indicate if you've ever gone bankrupt.

2. Capability: Not only must you have a good credit history, you also need the capability to pay your bills in the future. Experience helps. If you've worked in the industry in which you plan to start your business, your banker will feel more confident in your ability to succeed.

3. Capital: Your banker will feel more disposed to extending a loan to your company if you've already invested your own money in your enterprise. A banker will also examine the way in which you treat your company's profits. If you reinvest most of them in your business, you'll be more likely to obtain a loan than if you put all your company's profits in your pocket.

4. Circumstances: The circumstances of your business include such things as the health of the industry in which you operate, the state of the economy, and the impact of the economy on your business. If your endeavour can weather tough times, you'll more likely succeed in obtaining a loan than if your business is vulnerable to boom and bust cycles.

5. Coverage: A lender will want reassurance that a loan can be repaid even if something happens to you, your partners, or your facilities. This means you need insurance.

6. Cash flow: A cash-flow analysis will indicate your ability to repay a loan according to a regular schedule. It will also reassure your banker that you can operate your business without any surprises. All this information will help you and your banker to negotiate an appropriate loan for your business and an appropriate repayment schedule as well.

7. Collateral: In return for a loan, a lender may require a guarantee in the form of your personal property such as stocks, bonds, or real estate. The lender may accept security in the form of machinery or inventory. With certain kinds of loans, a lender will accept accounts receivable as a guarantee. You should make sure you're prepared to forfeit your security if you can't repay the loan.

MOST ENTREPRENEURS LIKE THEIR BANKS

According to a study of more than 200 bankers and 400 owner/managers, more than two-thirds of small-business clients are satisfied with their banking relationships. Although most small businesses borrow $100,000 or less, bank executives regard the small-business community as an important and profitable customer segment, and they all want to expand their share of the market.

The bad news? Almost one-third of small-business borrowers were dissatisfied with their banking relationships. They complained about high turnover among account managers and a lack of understanding among bankers of the nature of their specific business.

Entrepreneurs themselves did not understand that banks provide low-risk financing. They did not do enough to keep their bankers informed about changes in their businesses, nor did they even understand the terms of their loans. Finally, most owner/managers had little or no training in financial management and gave a low priority to the financial operations of their firms.

Keep a Clean Credit Record

With the development and application of new technologies, Canadian banks can now process a small-business loan application within hours. The application itself is no more than a page long, whether the applicant needs $1,000 or $30,000.

Banks rely on a combination of techniques to provide such service. One is called credit scoring. Comparing the applicant's household income, the annual sales of the applicant's business, and other information with a standardized database of customer profiles, the bank can determine the risk that the applicant might default on the loan.

Credit scoring works by evaluating patterns of behaviour of groups of customers and measuring risk accordingly. Using this approach, a lender can determine the precise level of risk involved in a particular loan, without evaluating the individual behaviour of each member of the group. If the applicant's score is sufficiently high, the bank can approve the loan within a single day.

Credit-scoring provides benefits for borrowers, as well.

1. It drastically reduces the amount of paperwork and information required on a loan application. In fact, for unsecured loans of up to $35,000, lenders require only a single page of information.
2. It reduces the time required to process a loan application. Most applications can be processed in a single day.
3. Lending decisions become more equitable as individual characteristics about the borrower become less significant. If your credit history is sound and you meet the expectations of the lender, you can anticipate receiving a loan, even if your particular company operates in an unusual industry.

Before they approve a loan, banks still evaluate an applicant's business and personal credit history. For more information on credit bureaus and your credit rating, see Chapter Two (page 34).

How Not to Get a Bank Loan

1. Don't specify the amount you need or its purpose.
2. Submit vague financial estimates about your business.
3. Don't invest any of your own money in your business.
4. Don't provide a personal guarantee.
5. Use commercial real estate as collateral but refuse to co-operate with an environmental assessment.
6. Walk in cold to a bank, demand a loan, but tell the banker that you'd prefer to keep your personal accounts at another institution.

BANKING IN A NUTSHELL

"We're like Hertz Rent-a-Car. When they rent you a car, they charge you for usage, and they expect to get the car back. When we give you a loan, we charge interest, and we expect to get our money back."

Roger Smith, President, Silicon Valley Bank

THE BUSINESS DEVELOPMENT BANK OF CANADA

The federal government administers a bank whose mandate specifically focuses on small Canadian companies.

Formerly called the Federal Business Development Bank (FBDB), now called the Business Development Bank of Canada (BDC), this bank provides counselling, consulting, and information, as well as financing to small companies.

Although its executives argue to the contrary, the bank is often considered a lender of last resort, providing funds to companies that no other bank in the country would approve. In its previous incarnation, the BDC did carry an extremely high ratio of bad loans on its books. But it has cleaned up its act, and it now provides a useful service to Canadian entrepreneurs.

In addition to financing, the BDC helps entrepreneurs with preparing a business plan, cash-flow forecasting, and budgeting. It also provides a consulting service to help entrepreneurs run their companies.

SMALL BUSINESSES LOANS ACT REVISED: IT'S DESIGNED FOR YOU

Under the Small Businesses Loans Act (SBLA), the federal government will guarantee most of a loan extended to a qualified small business. This eliminates most of the risk to the bank. Recent revisions to the SBLA have made bank financing even more accessible to small companies in Canada.

The maximum SBLA loan is now $250,000. The program now includes start-up companies as well as most for-profit enterprises with annual revenues of less than $5 million. SBLA loans can now be used to cover 90% (down from 100%) of the cost of purchasing land and new and used equipment and of purchasing, renovating, and improving a company's facilities.

For banks, the SBLA program carries no more risk than a conventional lending program. The minimum charge is a rate of 1 3/4% over prime to a maximum of 3% over prime or the current residential mortgage rate plus one, and the government will guarantee 85%. To secure the loan, a bank can take a charge against property or equipment, although personal guarantees are limited to 25% of the original loan. The fee for this guarantee is 2% of the original loan amount.

DEBT-EQUITY RECONSIDERED

Lenders usually have a list of criteria for identifying good prospective clients. One of the criteria high on their list is a low debt-equity ratio. Typically, lenders want the total debt-equity ratio to be no more than 2 after the proceeds of the loan are incorporated into the balance sheet. Most successful big businesses have debt-equity ratios of 2 or less, and lenders expect the same of a small business, no matter how unlikely it seems. In fact, blind application of the debt-equity ratio criteria to a business in the early phase of its existence can threaten its survival.

Nevertheless, in the initial stages of your business, there will be times when your equity, or net worth, is negative. This makes it impossible to establish a debt-equity ratio. Even when your company's net worth rises above zero, the ratio remains astonishingly high. In such a situation, debt financing is out of the question.

This will likely infuriate you, because you've already established that your business has the capability to survive. You've spent your resources carefully, counting every nickel and dime, and succeeded in making it through the start-up stage. Now your customers are beginning to pay you, money is trickling in, and more customers are knocking at your door. You hope to catch the momentum, take advantage of opportunities, and build on your success. But without money, you can't do it; not today, not tomorrow, maybe never.

For a considerable period, at least, you'll have to generate earnings and pay down debt to get your net equity on the balance sheet up to a reasonable sum that's acceptable to most bankers and investors. Before you can finance further expansion, you have to earn back your start-up losses.

As John Welsh and Jerry White, two U.S. consultants and authors, observe in comparing small companies with large, acquiring additional equity when a company is still recovering its start-up losses is extremely difficult. "The original investors have watched their holdings dwindle from the losses of the start-up period," Welsh and White say. "Now they want their capital returned before allowing other investors to reap the benefits. Also, original investors have often paid steep prices for their ownership. The offering price to new investors will likely be lower since it must be based on the current financial statements."

This is the point where the true mettle of your investors is tested. They become wary and skeptical of your promises. They've seen you spend their money; now they want some of it back, and they want to see a return on their investment, as well. Welsh and White call this "investor fatigue." Sometimes, your original investors may make demands that work contrary to the best interests of the company. Just when you need their patience and indulgence more than ever, they run out of patience and refuse to indulge you for another moment.

As we've discussed in the last chapter, you can take measures to improve your debt-equity ratio, not just by increasing earnings but by increasing profit margins, for example, through expense reduction, improved productivity, or higher prices.

VENTURE CAPITAL

Venture capitalists, as their name implies, put their own financial well-being at some risk to provide financing to entrepreneurs. Most of them will tell you that they make money on only two of every ten deals they complete. Of the other eight, five are mediocre at best; and two collapse before they ever get off the ground.

Perhaps because the odds of success seem so slim, venture capitalists demand a great deal in return for their investment. They may lose money on their two dead investments, but they seldom lose in a big way. Only the entrepreneur enjoys that dubious privilege.

As an entrepreneur, you might think that venture capital provides the answer to your dreams. Unlike a bank loan, you don't necessarily have to put up your house, your car, your spouse and child, and so on as security. Unlike your friends and relatives, venture capitalists don't demand a detailed explanation about how you're spending their life savings. All you have to do is get down to business and build your company—quickly—sharing the eventual profits with your investors.

Venture capitalists keep a close eye on their investments, so you'll likely spend every day of the week talking to them. And you'll have to start generating profits quickly, because most venture capitalists are not patient investors. They want to get in and out of a deal as quickly as they can.

Only you can determine whether this is the route for you. Here are some other characteristics of venture capitalists.

1. Venture capitalists seldom invest in start-up companies. They want to kick the tires, examine your track record, and watch a business in operation so they can catch a glimpse of its potential before they put their money behind it.

2. Venture capitalists never invest in a business without demanding a lot in return. If you think you can use the money of a venture capitalist and still retain most of your business, you're wrong. You'll likely lose control of the business, temporarily, at least, as the venture capitalist watches you turn your business into a profitable operation. But as the saying goes, 10% of a profitable business is better than 100% of nothing.

3. Once you've accepted financing from a venture capitalist, you should be prepared to relinquish control of your company altogether at some date in the future, usually within five to seven years. Eventually you'll have to take the company public or sell out to a bigger company. That's how venture capitalists cash out. So if you intend to start a business that you can leave lock, stock, and barrel to your grandchildren or that will provide you with a nice, steady income for the next couple of decades, don't get involved with venture capitalists unless you're sure you can buy them out when the business becomes successful.

4. Venture capitalists are not silent partners. They'll monitor your performance closely and demand to see detailed evidence that your business is moving toward its goals.

5. Venture capitalists usually specialize in particular industries, which offer high potential for growth. High technology is still popular with venture capitalists; grocery stores are not.

THE BENEFITS OF VENTURE CAPITAL

In addition to placing demands on an entrepreneur, venture capitalists bring some benefits to a company. Most venture capitalists have strong business backgrounds, often in finance, management, and accounting. Few entrepreneurs have these skills at their fingertips.

By the nature of their business, venture capitalists maintain an extensive network of contacts within the business community. They can help an entrepreneur with marketing, product development, and other areas of a growing business.

Venture capitalists bring discipline to a business that you might not muster on your own. If you have no one but yourself to report to, you can always put off till tomorrow the number-crunching you should have done today. Venture capitalists demand action, when it's required.

Business professionals in your community, such as lawyers, accountants, and management consultants, can refer you to venture capitalists. Your local chamber of commerce or board of trade can likely help you, as well.

Before you approach a potential venture investor, you'll need a detailed business plan and evidence that the plan actually works. They'll want to see your projections about the business but, more importantly, they'll want to understand how you intend to meet those projections.

With this in mind, they'll want to meet your management team, check your financial condition, and meet your suppliers and customers.

GOVERNMENT FUNDING AND OTHER SERVICES

Most of the provincial governments in Canada operate extremely efficient services that can provide you with an extensive library of useful booklets, brochures, and regulatory guidelines for entrepreneurs. Most of them operate consulting services, as well.

Some governments provide financial assistance to companies that hire employees with particular skills. Some will provide loan guarantees to help companies in specific industries with their expansion plans.

Governments also operate programs that will cover the cost of seeking export opportunities, enhancing your company's technological expertise, and hiring young people or participating in college and university co-op programs.

To find out more about these programs, check with some of your fellow entrepreneurs. Go to your chamber of commerce or board of trade and ask a few questions about the program. Your local library also carries several publications that list sources of provincial and federal government financing.

GOING PUBLIC

In the early stages of your business, issuing shares in your company on a stock exchange is seldom an option for raising cash. We'll deal with the details of going public in Chapter 10.

financing
continued

8

An entrepreneur has little control over the total amount of capital invested in her company, unless she tries to raise additional capital—a time-consuming, arduous, and in some cases fruitless, procedure. The entrepreneur has much greater control over profits. By increasing profits, she can raise the company's return on investment (ROI), a figure that all investors look at closely before and after they make an investment. Improvements in ROI, however, often require additional funds, which many small companies cannot easily acquire.

An entrepreneur may have pricing in place to generate a healthy pretax profit; new orders on the books to keep the operation busy for several months; and the cost of labour and materials under control. To improve ROI, she might try to increase sales—and profits—by offering credit terms of net 30 days. Although sales might increase, such a manoeuvre can also have a negative effect on cash flow and require the company to use its overdraft for a prolonged period until payments are received. Although investors might be pleased with the improved ROI, lenders frown on such a situation, no matter how confident the entrepreneur might be that her customers will eventually pay their bills.

Fortunately, her suppliers can help. Materials often account for a large portion of monthly expenses. By taking advantage of volume discounts, for example, and discounts for prompt payment, a company can reduce its expenses and improve operating results. Once again, however, the entrepreneur requires additional financing to purchase materials in the volumes required to take advantage of the discounts. "In such a situation, each move to improve ROI results in trading liquidity for profit," observe U.S. consultants John Welsh and Jerry F. White. "Thus, additional financing through debt or equity or a combination of the two [is] required."

In this case, a number of variables influence the financial condition of the company.

GETTING PAID BY THE CUSTOMER

After providing goods to a customer, the entrepreneur bills the customer and waits for payment, incurring some risk and uncertainty in the process. No matter how large the contract, it's worthless unless the customer pays. To alleviate uncertainty, the entrepreneur can make informal inquiries to other companies that might have done business with the customer. She can make more formal inquiries through a credit bureau or join a credit service that provides credit histories, for a fee.

Alternatively, she can ask the customer for payment in advance or sell her receivables at a discount to a third party. This option makes sense only if the entrepreneur needs cash immediately. Otherwise, the discount far exceeds the value of the relief provided by relinquishing responsibility for collecting unpaid bills. Also, companies that buy receivables place restrictions on the age and creditworthiness of the invoices in question.

CREDIT TERMS

If the entrepreneur sells on credit, she doesn't make a profit until she collects the payment. Meanwhile, she has to finance the cost of the unpaid bill. Banks, meanwhile, will not lend against receivables that have been outstanding for more than 90 days.

To encourage prompt payment and avoid extended delays, the company needs a defined credit policy. The policy will depend on industry practices, the entrepreneur's need for cash, and other factors. It will cover the length of time for which the company will allow a customer to delay a payment before charging interest, and set the rate of interest, as well. It will also set the discount for early payment.

The credit policy may also extend to asking the customer for a purchase order before the company starts work or ships the order. It can also define conditions when installment payments or a letter of credit issued by the customer may be in order.

THE INVOICE

A company's credit and payment policies will determine the specific appearance and scope of its invoices. In general, however, an invoice should contain:

- The company name, address, phone and fax numbers, and e-mail address
- GST or Business Number
- Customer's name and address
- Purchase order number, if applicable
- Invoice number and date
- A description of the product or service
- The amount owing, with GST and PST shown separately
- Payment terms
- Personalized memo (e.g., "Thanks for your business")

CONTROLLING RECEIVABLES

An entrepreneur should know precisely how much his customers owe and for how long they've owed it. Depending on industry practice, accounts generally become overdue after 30, 60, or 90 days. When they do, the entrepreneur has to initiate a collection procedure. Sometimes a simple phone call will work. You might also suggest a payment schedule to the customer to accommodate his cash flow. Never ignore an overdue account. Like everyone else, your customers will pay the supplier who demands it most insistently.

You might hesitate to jeopardize a relationship with a customer who hasn't paid his bill. But how much does a customer contribute to your business if he doesn't pay you? If you decide to maintain a relationship with the customer, try to incorporate a fee for the late payment into your next bill.

PUTTING EXCESS CASH TO WORK

If your business generates cash, it indicates good health. However, you have to put your cash to work. Once you've paid your bills and met your other financial obligations such as taxes and payroll, you should put any extra money in an interest-bearing account or use it to pay down loans or mortgages. Some banks offer accounts that automatically shift surplus funds to your loan. Whatever you do, don't just let it sit there or spend it on a new car.

MAKING PAYMENTS

You want your customers to pay you as quickly as possible. At the same time, you want to extend your payables over the longest possible period. This gives you immediate use of your customers' cash, and lets you take full advantage of your own cash before you transfer it to a supplier.

Most businesses still use cheques to pay suppliers. Cheques help you to keep track of your cash flow. Cheques often clear for payment on the same day as they're deposited so you should make sure your current account has enough money in it to cover outstanding cheques. You should also reconcile your account with cancelled cheques or pay your bank to provide this service for you. If you use cash, ask for a receipt. Without one, you can't claim the expense for tax purposes.

As an alternative to cash or cheques, you can use credit cards or preauthorized payments. Business credit cards can be used by authorized employees to cover business and travel expenses. You pay a fee on an annual or transactional basis. But the fee is often worth the convenience, because the cards simplify record-keeping. With business credit cards, you can set predetermined authorization limits and take advantage of a period of free credit by paying the balance in full by the due date.

You can also arrange for recurring payments such as insurance and mortgage payments to be transferred automatically each month from your account to a supplier's account, either directly with your insurance or mortgage company or through your bank.

TRADE CREDIT

When a supplier gives you 30 days to pay, she's giving you 30 days of trade credit. Trade credit is the largest category of short-term debt. Small businesses rely heavily on it. But if you abuse it, suppliers may refuse credit altogether and ask for cash on delivery. Not only do you lose the convenience and benefits of credit, you could also jeopardize your credit rating. Trade credit is really a short-term loan, and many suppliers check your credit rating before they'll extend credit to you.

LEASING

Leasing converts a capital expenditure into an operating expense. Owner/managers often choose to lease their company's office equipment, trucks, and company cars. By leasing the equipment, they can often obtain 100% financing while preserving their credit lines and protecting themselves against technological obsolescence. Fixed monthly costs also act as an effective hedge against inflation, and payments are, in most cases, tax deductible.

Companies also lease manufacturing and warehouse equipment, taking advantage of competitive interest rates offered by equipment suppliers. Among other things, leasing enables them to test the latest technologies without making an irreversible commitment.

Leasing comes at a cost, however. You'll end up paying more for the equipment than you'd pay if you bought it outright. But the benefits sometimes outweigh the costs, especially if your company needs cash or has to maintain a clean balance sheet to keep lenders and investors happy.

Also, the tax benefits of leasing are somewhat overrated. You can write off monthly lease expenses as long as they're reasonable. But if you buy the same item, you can write off a fixed amount for depreciation each year. In fact, for some items, such as computers, Revenue Canada allows a relatively high depreciation rate and additional tax benefits when you sell the equipment, making purchasing more attractive than leasing.

However, a lease sometimes brings cash-flow advantages that you can't get if you buy an item outright. A lease generally requires little or no money down, for example. Likewise, if your company is already heavily in debt, you may not be able to borrow more money. Instead, you can go to a leasing company, which will lend you the money under other terms to obtain the same asset.

Leasing also lets you use an asset without worrying that it will become obsolete. You can lease the item for a couple of years, then give it back and lease a newer model.

With a pure lease, you're actually renting the item for a long term. Ownership resides with the lessor, and the owner may be responsible for maintenance and ultimate disposal. Other leases, however, are really just loans by another name, with an agreement to purchase at the end of the loan's term. There's a difference, for tax purposes, between one type of lease and another, and you should check with your accountant to make sure you select the arrangement that makes the most sense under your particular circumstances.

RISK MANAGEMENT

A corporation practises financial risk management to increase value, through increasing expected net cash flows; by reducing the cost of capital; or by protecting against change in asset/liability values. A well-executed financial risk management policy allows a company to stabilize its operating cash flow and reduce the probability of financial distress.

Most companies manage the financial risk inherent in interest-rate and foreign currency fluctuations using hedging programs. Properly executed, these programs are not speculative, but act as insurance against financial hazards, just as liability insurance protects a company against unforeseen accidents.

A company that imports or exports products, for example, is subject to fluctuations in currency values. Likewise, a company may have to price its goods or services in competition with foreign companies. A Japanese company, for example, may be able to sell its products more cheaply to your Canadian customers if the yen falls against the C$.

For entrepreneurs reluctant to get involved in currency speculation, a hedging program may seem risky. But it's far more risky for a company exposed to currency risk to do nothing. In fact, a company that imports or exports has already engaged in currency speculation. From one week to the next, the difference in value between the U.S. and Canadian dollars can fluctuate by 3%. That may seem insignificant, but it directly affects a company's bottom line. To a growing company, 3% can spell the difference between seizing an opportunity or letting it pass because of insufficient funds.

As Toronto treasury consultant John Whale points out, "Even though no one knows for sure what the future holds, a sound strategy and focus on the markets can generate rewards, even for the small player, with little risk. After all, saving $30,000 on a purchase of US$1 million is just as important for the smaller operation as saving $300,000 for the larger one with US$10 million to buy."

Once a company has reached even the modest exposures of, say, $10 million a year in foreign currency flows, Whale says, it can benefit enormously from a sound currency management strategy, employing instruments and trading techniques that are usually used by larger, more sophisticated participants. Because no one can really be sure of the direction of foreign-exchange rates, companies of all sizes must pay attention to daily market movements. They can also develop strategies to address corporate-governance issues regarding risk tolerance, credit, and compliance. Once the strategy is in place, it needs to be executed and monitored continually.

HEDGING IN ACTION

In an article written for *Canadian Treasurer* magazine, consultant John Whale cites the example of an importer and distributor of furniture from the U.S. The company has analyzed the possible effects of currency movements on its business in the areas of product-pricing competitiveness, labour costs, and accounting policies. It can include a cushion for exchange-rate movements in its pricing, but the owner was concerned that the company was leaving money on the table by not managing its exposures professionally.

In September 1996, when the company sought professional advice, the US$/C$ spot rate was 1.3650. Based on news stories, the company strongly believed that the C$ was likely to strengthen. Its US$ needs were roughly $1million per month to the end of the year. With the pricing cushion

(approximately 1.3750 at the time) in place on booked ship-
ments, the company was willing to take some risk on half its
exposure ($2 million) versus what it could easily lock in
straight away. It hedged the other half immediately.

The company then put in place a very simple strategy: It
put in a buy stop with its bankers at 1.3700 and continued
to move the level down as the C$ actually did strengthen. It
funded its cash requirements in the interim with short-term
swaps.

By the time the rate reached its low of 1.3270 in early
November, the company's stop was resting at 1.3350.
Believing that it would continue, the company decided on a
target of 1.3200. Given that the rate had moved so far in
such a short time, Whale advised the company to write
1.3200 US$ puts (C$ calls). These were, at the time, in-the-
money for each of the company's maturity dates, so it earned
a healthy premium.

Ideally the company would have exercised the options
and lived happily ever after. But this is real life, and history
tells us that 1.3270 was the recent low for the US$. The
market moved up sharply from there. The company was
stopped out at 1.3350 and bought back the puts for a small
gain. However, the company increased its bottom line by
more than $60,000, having risked the opportunity cost of
$10,000 (the original stop of 1.3700 versus the then-market
of 1.3650). Meanwhile, it increased its knowledge of the market and simple trading techniques enormously.

advisers

9

Far more than a large organization, a new company will rely heavily on its advisers to see it through the difficult years of its growth. Chosen with care, accountants, lawyers, financial advisers, and management consultants can all contribute new ideas and much-needed solutions to problems that the entrepreneur can't solve on his own. Likewise, a well-chosen board of directors can bring new perspectives to the entrepreneur's long-range planning, while making sure that the organization remains focused on its goals and objectives.

THE ACCOUNTANT

Entrepreneurs often have expertise in a particular field, which they've learned during their careers as corporate employees. But the best entrepreneur acknowledges his shortcomings and seeks counsel from other experts to complement his skills.

In many cases, an entrepreneur has only a general understanding of the financial issues involved in starting and building a company. An accountant can provide many of the critical skills required to keep an organization's financial house in order.

In addition to accounting, auditing, and tax services, accountants can also offer good advice on other aspects of starting and running a business.

At the very least, they can show an entrepreneur how to set up a company's accounting system to generate the information required to meet its tax obligations. They can also present their ideas on the best structure for the business and help the entrepreneur define his market. Through their own network of contacts, they can identify potential sources of appropriate financing for the business. Accountants usually know something about employee compensation plans and the structuring of partnership or shareholder agreements.

Some accountants specialize in particular aspects of business, such as buying and selling a business, business valuations, strategic planning, risk management, insolvency, and bankruptcy. Even in providing tax services, an accountant can attend to far more than a company's year-end tax returns. For the entrepreneur, whose business and personal lives are inextricably intertwined, accountants can advise on estate planning, compensation plans, and retirement planning. At the appropriate time, they can also help the entrepreneur expand the company through an acquisition or harvest his assets by selling the business.

To find an accountant who's knowledgeable about small-business issues, the obvious place to go first is another entrepreneur. Colleagues and business acquaintances can help, as well. The right candidate will not only speak your language and understand the issues involved in building a company, she will also understand the personal issues that affect your business decisions. As a result, you should find someone with whom you can share details about your personal as well as your business life. An accountant can only help you plan your retirement, for example, if he knows your family and marital status and your long-term personal aspirations.

TEN QUESTIONS TO ASK YOUR ACCOUNTANT

When interviewing chartered accountants to determine who will best meet your needs, be sure to ask the following 10 key questions:

1. Why should I pick your firm over any other?
2. Does your firm focus on any particular industry or geographic region?

3. How many offices and partners do you have? That is, are you local, regional, or national?

4. What experience have you had in my industry? How many clients like me do you serve currently and can I call a few for references?

5. How do you bill for your services—as the job progresses or once it's completed? Do you need a retainer? What is the fee range for jobs such as mine?

6. Who will work on my assignment? If other staff members, what is their experience?

7. Do you have access to other specialists if I have special needs outside your area of expertise?

8. Are you using the latest technology to ensure that work is done efficiently and at the lowest cost? For example, do you e-file tax returns?

9. What specific services do you offer?

10. Will you be there for me whenever I need you?

Source: The Institute of Chartered Accountants of Ontario

THE LAWYER

All lawyers are not alike, and even the best lawyer doesn't know everything. While a general practitioner can take care of most of your routine legal requirements, from helping you incorporate your business to drawing up a will, you should hire a specialist in some situations.

A labour lawyer, for example, can advise you on employment-related issues. A litigation lawyer can help you collect overdue accounts. Some lawyers specialize in computer law, others in contract law, trusts, or estates. Make sure you hire the right lawyer for the job.

There are several ways to find a good lawyer.

1. Ask a friend or associate: Like the first rule of marketing, the first rule of professional referrals is, "Talk to people you know."

   If the person understands your business and your legal predicament—and if you trust the person's judgment—you stand a good chance of finding a lawyer who can deal with your problem effectively.

2. The Canadian Bar Association (CBA): The CBA operates a referral service for lawyers, categorized by specialty. If you want a lawyer experienced in labour law, for example, you can ask the CBA to provide you with a few names. Then you can make an appointment to meet each of them, assess their skill and competence, and choose the one you like. (The initial interview doesn't cost much.)

3. Each provincial law society also has referral services.

Lawyers charge up to $250 per hour for their services. In downtown law firms in Toronto, Vancouver, and other large cities, they charge even more.

What do you get in return? If you're lucky, you'll get excellent service, informative and perceptive insights, clear explanations of your options, and a satisfactory result, for which you'll gladly pay a reasonable fee.

If you're unlucky, you'll get a lesson in incompetence, delivered by a pompous youth in an expensive suit, at an outrageous fee that will leave you more angry than you were when you first contacted the lawyer.

Other lawyers charge a contingency fee of 25% to 40% of the amount involved. Cases involving lawsuits and collections of overdue accounts are often billed in this fashion. The contingency agreement must be in writing. In some provinces, this arrangement isn't legal. But your bill will equal an equivalent amount anyway.

Depending on the complexity of the issues involved, some lawyers will charge a retainer that reassures them that they will be compensated for their time. This retainer is fair; after all, the lawyer has to be compensated for his time and, if he doesn't know you, he can't be sure you'll pay him after he's finished the work. Even lawyers have to deal with deadbeats.

THE CONSULTANT

Pressed for time and often operating in isolation, dealing with issues that cover the entire spectrum of management, an entrepreneur often needs advice but seldom gets the right kind.

Entrepreneurs frequently turn to friends and associates for assistance. But friends and associates usually have neither the skill nor the authority to provide sound, direct judgments about an entrepreneur's business. They often couch their advice in friendly terms or provide generalized observations based on their own limited knowledge of the business and its operations, when the entrepreneur really needs solid, unequivocal, and sometimes sobering advice.

Other professionals, such as lawyers and accountants, can provide assistance as well. But they often don't have the time, expertise, or commitment to help the entrepreneur over the long term or with a specific management issue. Even a board of directors can't focus on the day-to-day issues with which an entrepreneur needs help to identify, address, and resolve a particular issue.

Consultants, on the other hand, can bring their skills to bear on specific issues. They must be chosen with care, and their skills must be matched to the problems at hand. But often their advice is worth its weight in gold. As the Association of Consulting Management Engineers Inc. has observed, not without a touch of self-interest, "The most frequent users of consultants are usually the most successful companies. The most progressive-minded managements are constantly seeking more effective ways of managing their businesses."

Consultants can be useful for such things as developing more scientific ways of organizing and operating a company. They can bring new methods of marketing and production into a company's operations. Human resource consultants can improve a company's personnel recruitment and training procedures, often a critical issue for a growing firm. Consultants can also help an entrepreneur develop and establish long-range planning techniques to maximize future opportunities.

Entrepreneurs frequently hesitate to hire consultants, however, for many reasons. Concern about high fees, a reluctance to reveal proprietary methods and procedures, reservations about the consultant's knowledge of the business, and apprehension about personality clashes rank high on the list.

Many of these issues can be resolved by selecting a consultant through a process of referral. Friends, professional advisers, and others can often suggest potential candiates to provide the specific consulting services a company needs to progress. Especially if these advisers work with many small companies themselves, they'll likely know of consultants who have worked well with growing organizations such as yours.

THE FINANCIAL PLANNER

Because your personal and business interests are so closely related, a financial planner can help you set the personal financial objectives that you want to reach by building a business. You may want tips on tax saving strategies, life-insurance advice, or guidance in selecting mutual funds. You may be aiming to finance a university education for your daughter or planning your retirement or your estate. In all these cases, a good financial planner can help.

Financial planners earn their money by remaining up-to-date on the forces at work in the financial world. Entrepreneurs seldom have time to pay attention to these forces, nor can they inform themselves about the multitude of investment vehicles available to help them achieve their personal financial goals.

A financial planner can keep you informed about your investment options, answering questions like:

- Is the market cheap or expensive?
- Which mutual funds should I buy?
- Where can I get the highest rates of return?
- How can I save on my taxes?
- What is my investment comfort level?

Many financial planners also sell mutual funds and life insurance, and some will even negotiate a home mortgage for you. Unfortunately, the profession is unregulated, and anyone can call himself a financial planner, even if he can't calculate his own age.

To avoid mistakes—and bad planning—look for a Certified Financial Planner. These people put the initials C.F.P. after their names. Anyone with a C.F.P. designation has studied extensively and passed certified exams. The Canadian Association of Financial Planners can help you find a reputable financial planner.

An independent financial planner can provide you with the best products offered by many different companies. Financial planners who work for a single company generally limit themselves to selling their own company's products.

A financial planner may charge you nothing at all and be worth no more. If the planner doesn't get results, then his advice isn't worth much.

But a planner who helps you earn a profit on your money, year after year, earns his fees.

Financial planners bill their clients in one of two general ways:

1. Fee only. The planner charges a one-time flat fee of $\frac{1}{2}$% to 1% of your portfolio. But you usually need at least $50,000 to invest.

   The planner may also charge an hourly fee.

2. Commission only. The financial planner gets paid only when she sells one of her financial products. The financial planner is compensated either by a commission paid directly by you (usually 3% to 5% of the amount invested) or by a mutual fund company in the form of a finder's fee.

   This is by far the most popular method of paying a financial planner.

THE DIRECTOR

A board of directors can provide an entrepreneur with long-term vision, guidance, and counsel. Often, however, an entrepreneur appoints the wrong people to the board. Family members, professional advisers, bankers, and inside managers often feel reluctant to jeopardize their personal or professional relationships with the company. As a result, they feel reluctant to give their unqualified opinion about issues that might bring offence to the entrepreneur. Obviously, they can provide only limited guidance.

For best results, a board must include some outside directors who have no stake in the success or failure of the company other than their own professional pride. These individuals bring their experience and skills to bear on the evolution of the company, but have no vested interest in its success.

Organizations of all sizes have difficulty finding good directors. But small companies can improve their prospects by looking for likely candidates among mid-level managers in large corporations. These individuals usually haven't acquired the expertise or reputation required by the board of larger organizations. But they have ambition and experience in their particular field, and they often have a solid and well-grounded knowledge of business processes.

University professors, retired executives, institutional administrators, and management consultants can help, as well.

Informal surveys show that only about 50% of small companies compensate their board of directors. Some pay an annual retainer and a small fee for attending each board meeting. Family-owned companies are less likely than companies owned by small groups of shareholders to pay their board members a fee.

The role of the board varies from company to company. A survey by the U.S. Conference Board indicated that directors usually deal with long-range corporate objectives; corporate strategies; allocation of major resources; major financial decisions; mergers; acquisitions, and divestments; performance appraisals of top managers; succession; and compensation.

These are all potentially sensitive issues, so it's important for an entrepreneur to attract strong and independent voices to the board if it is to have any impact on the company's future success. The entrepreneur who appoints overly agreeable people to his board will get the advice he deserves. As management consultant Peter Drucker says, companies need the kind of board member "who makes sure that there is effective top management; who makes sure that management thinks and plans; who serves as the conscience of the institution; as the counsel, adviser, and informed critic of top management."

In appointing directors, an entrepreneur has to admit that he's relinquishing authority. Good directors will also be good critics. Although they offer their views in a constructive spirit, they may offend the entrepreneur who has come to see himself as king of the company. In fact, for this reason alone, a board of directors serves a valid purpose simply by reminding the entrepreneur of his own fallibility.

Your directors may insist upon putting a policy of director's liability insurance in place to limit their exposure to certain kinds of liability. While this type of insurance isn't necessarily expensive, it can be difficult to get, and the insurance company may ask a lot of personal and business questions before agreeing to put such a policy in place.

putting
it
all together

10

As your business becomes established you'll face a number of decisions that will determine the path you follow in years to come. Many of these decisions will depend on the personal aspirations that you identified before you started the business. Your various needs and desires will all influence the decisions you make about running your business. Sometimes your decisions will be influenced by factors beyond your control. Your health may suffer, for example, as a result of the incessant pressure of building a company. Your family may demand more of your time. Despite your best efforts, your business may not succeed.

In this chapter, we'll explore some of the options from which you can choose as your business evolves. We'll also discuss some of the ways that you can convert the equity you've contributed to the business into cash. Finally, we'll discuss the pros and cons of involving family members in the business as you plan for succession.

EXPANDING YOUR BUSINESS

Some entrepreneurs feel happy with a business that provides them with steady, dependable income and a place where they can apply their management and business skills. They have no desire to build an empire c make a lasting mark on the world. Nor do they want to spend every waking hour dealing with their business. They have other interests, and they enjoy balancing business with pleasure.

For other entrepreneurs, business and pleasure are synonymous. They can't think of anything they'd rather do than work at building their company. They eat, sleep, think, and dream about their business. They value all other aspects of their lives primarily for their contribution to their business success.

Entrepreneurs in the first category have little interest in working night and day to expand their companies. Entrepreneurs in the second category think of little else. As their business becomes established, they look for ways to expand it and for the financing to support their aspirations. To avoid mistakes, however, they take a methodical and prudent approach to expansion.

Expansion takes a number of different forms. It may include:

1. Geographical expansion: Opening a plant or sales office in another city, province, or country
2. Expansion of production capacity: Adding equipment or replacing old machinery with newer, faster technology
3. Adding products or services: Extending an existing line or starting a new one
4. Merging with another company: Adding capacity and resources and possibly expanding geographically in the process
5. Buying another company: Adding capacity and eliminating a competitor in the process
6. Franchising: Another way of expanding your market
7. Changing the focus of the business: Identifying key areas of the operation that generate most of your sales and focusing on them

PROS AND CONS OF EXPANSION

As we've mentioned, expansion has advantages and disadvantages. The advantages include:

- Increased sales, which may lead to increased profits (although this isn't guaranteed),
- Competitive advantages,
- Greater challenges from managing a larger enterprise,
- Increased recognition, and
- Stimulation of focused growth.

Against these advantages, you have to weigh several disadvantages, including:

- The risk of losses caused by expansion,
- The confusion and mistakes that occur when operating in new areas,
- Need for delegation and relinquishing control,
- Additional demands on your time,
- Disruption of routines and distraction from core business caused by additional activities,
- Competitive disadvantages caused by stretching your resources, and
- Possibility of competition with customers or suppliers.

PLANNING FOR EXPANSION

If you decide to proceed with expansion, you should proceed methodically and consider the following procedures:

1. Evaluate and revise your business and marketing plans.
2. Calculate the financial requirements of expansion and determine where you'll find the necessary funding.
3. Evaluate your managers and employees to identify key personnel to carry out expansion plans.
4. Analyze the effect of expansion on your customers.
5. Analyze the effect of expansion on your family and personal life.
6. Reexamine your strengths and weaknesses.
7. Consult your advisers.

GOING PUBLIC

Whether you're expanding your business, building its revenues and profits, or establishing its presence in existing markets, raising money by issuing shares to the public is an option for companies of sufficient size and profitability.

In fact, many entrepreneurs and the investors who back them look forward to the day when they can list their companies on one of Canada's stock exchanges, issue shares to the public, and watch the value of their company (and their own net worth) rise ever higher.

The dream seldom includes the sleepless nights, the ulcers, the heated arguments, and the suicidal thoughts that come with taking a company public. We'll deal with these more personal aspects of business growth later in this chapter.

In making a public share offering, companies rarely proceed until they have an established track record. Unless the market for new issues is particularly hot, start-up companies should look elsewhere for funding.

Even for established companies, the process can be excruciating: It's time-consuming, expensive, and complex. And though you may think that a public offering will bring you closer to the pot of gold at the end of the rainbow, it doesn't always make you or your company wealthier.

TYPES OF PUBLIC OFFERING

There are two general types of public offering: primary and secondary.

A primary offering involves the sale of unissued securities to the public. In return, the company receives the capital.

A secondary offering involves the sale of securities belonging to the owners of the company, who then receive the proceeds.

You can also combine the two types of offering. In fact, most initial public offerings are primary offerings. Investors like to see their money put to good use, expanding the company, for example, so they stand a chance of reaping a reward for their risk.

For obvious reasons, investors shy away from secondary offerings, in which their money goes right into the pockets of a company's owners.

WHY GO PUBLIC?

Apart from the gratification it will bring to your own ego, you might have one or several good reasons for taking your company public. As usual in entrepreneurial deliberations, these reasons have aspects that pertain to your business and your personal life. They include:

1. Estate planning: Evaluating your shares in your company when you die is easier if they're publicly traded. There's also a much greater market for a company's shares if they're traded publicly.

2. Access to capital: A public offering gives you access to another source of capital. If you've exhausted your sources of debt, and your company can't generate more

capital on its own without expanding, then a public offering might be the solution to your problems.

3. Owner divestiture: If you currently hold most of your personal wealth in your company and you want to diversify your holdings, you can do it more easily after a public offering.

4. Employee incentive plans: Stock in a publicly held company provides an attractive incentive to executives to build the company further and keep it profitable.

WHY NOT GO PUBLIC?

There are personal and business reasons why you might choose not to take your company public. These include:

1. Short-term pressure: Once you go public, your shareholders will demand results every quarter. You'll no longer have the luxury of excusing poor performance in this quarter by saying that the prospects for the business look rosy two years ahead. Shareholders want performance now.

2. Confidentiality: Going public, as the term suggests, means you have to disclose to the public all sorts of information that you can keep to yourself in a private company, such as profits, losses, compensation, stock option programs, cost of sales, net income, and borrowings. If your company takes sick, everyone will know.

3. Accounting: To comply with securities regulations, your accounting systems have to address much more than the money you can save on your taxes.

4. Costs: In addition to the cost of the initial public offering, which can range as high as $200,000, you have to meet ongoing expenses such as periodic reports.

5. Dividends: You may not have to pay dividends in your first few years as a public company, but eventually shareholders will demand that you pay them.

CRITICAL SUPPORT FOR A PUBLIC OFFERING

In making a decision to take your company public, you should consult with your lawyer and accountant. If you decide to proceed, you'll need a legal adviser with expertise in securities law, an underwriter to help you structure the transaction and sell the shares to the public in return for a fee, an independent accountant, and a financial printer.

With their help, you'll determine your company's value, the number of shares you'll issue, and the percentage of ownership you'll relinquish. You'll satisfy securities regulators that you operate a legitimate business with reasonable prospects for future growth. You'll conduct dog-and-pony shows for securities analysts who will ask a lot of penetrating questions about why they should invest in your company. These individuals will spend as much time evaluating you and your capabilities as they will evaluating the company itself.

If all goes well, you'll make an Initial Public Offering, investors will buy your company's shares, and you'll enter a new stage of your company's life.

The actual value of your company's stock will depend on the powers of supply and demand. A stock is worth only what somebody else is willing to pay for it. When fifteen people all want to buy the stock and only one person wants to sell it, the stock price will rise. On the other side of the coin, when fifteen people want to sell a stock and only one wants to buy, the stock price will fall until the buyer agrees with the price.

In following a share's ups and downs, buyers and sellers pay close attention to corporate earnings. If earnings rise steadily, so does the stock price. When earnings fall, the stock price generally falls, too. Sometimes, however, a company's earnings go up as stock prices fall. Sometimes earnings will fall as stock prices go up.

ALTERNATIVES TO EXPANSION

Many entrepreneurs start their own business because they want a sense of independence and freedom from interference. This usually means freedom from marching to the beat of someone else's drummer. But as a small business grows, the entrepreneur inevitably becomes involved in other people's affairs. Unless you operate a one-person business, you'll add employees as you build your company. Employees make more demands on your time than any other aspect of a business. The larger your business grows, the more time you'll have to spend addressing other people's concerns, solving other people's problems, and depending on other people to help you achieve your goals. Ironically, you may get immersed in the very situations that inspired you to venture out on your own and start your own business in the first place.

As your business grows, you might also find yourself facing a number of personal challenges that you might not have anticipated at the outset. A study by U.S. consultants David Boyd and David Gumpert, for example, indicates that entrepreneurs pay an extremely high cost for the satisfaction they derive from building a successful company. At least once a week, up to 65% of the 450 entrepreneurs they surveyed reported suffering from back problems, indigestion, insomnia, or headaches. "To keep getting the satisfaction entrepreneurship brings," the authors say, "they appear willing to tolerate such evidence of stress."

Financial risk and financial satisfaction account for much of the anxiety and exhilaration of building a small business. Boyd and Gumpert found that most entrepreneurs thrive on these intense feelings. "What left the strongest impression on us was the depth and range of difficulties that entrepreneurs encounter on a daily basis and, paradoxically, the amount of pleasure they derive from this experience." In fact, only 2 of the 450 entrepreneurs they surveyed disagreed that a career in small business brings satisfaction and self-fulfillment. The rest said that entrepreneurship brings a multitude of benefits, including:

- Financial rewards
- Independence
- Freedom of decision-making
- Accountability to oneself
- A sense of achievement

Nevertheless, entrepreneurs pay a price for their enjoyment, primarily in the amount of stress they endure. Stress comes from a variety of sources, including loneliness and isolation, time constraints, problems with employees, and the need to achieve more.

Entrepreneurs surveyed by Boyd and Gumpert reported vague feelings of loneliness. "They all complained of spending so much time on their business that they had little left for family and friends. Indeed, in some cases, confusion existed in their minds about where their business lives ended and their personal lives began."

The long hours of business also prevent entrepreneurs from pursuing other activities, even if they can afford them. "It's one thing to be unable to take an exotic vacation because you can't afford it," Boyd and Gumpert point out. "It's another to be able to afford the trip but feel unable to take it because the business won't allow your absence."

Likewise, entrepreneurs feel frustrated and disappointed in their relationships with partners and subordinates. "They know precisely how they want their companies to function," say Boyd and Gumpert. "The problem is getting employees to make it happen." In many cases, entrepreneurs end up attending to details that they should have delegated, simply because they can't or won't rely on employees to do the work properly.

Finally, entrepreneurs all feel a need to achieve, which can add pressure to the life of an individual who has already achieved a considerable amount. "Company growth is a reflection of your overall ability," said one entrepreneur. If the company stops growing, it reflects poorly on the individual's ability, not just as an owner and manager but as a human being.

The stress arising from these sources often creates physical symptoms. But many entrepreneurs simply ignore them or accept them as the price of building a business. Instead of accepting these signs of stress, which can eventually lead to far more debilitating problems, an entrepreneur can take stock of her situation, find ways to relieve stress and enjoy life. Boyd and Gumpert suggest such mechanisms as

- Networking
- Vacations, even short breaks
- Better communication with subordinates
- Satisfaction outside the organization, through hobbies, civic activities, and so on
- Delegating

"If small business managers come to terms with stress, they can enhance their careers and lengthen their lives," the authors conclude.

REVISING YOUR PLAN

To relieve stress and change the way they spend their time, most entrepreneurs will have to revise their business and personal plans. After devoting several years to the growth and success of their business, they will have to determine once again exactly what they want to derive from their work and how they want it to contribute to their personal lives. In some cases they may decide to sell their business while its value is still sufficiently high to make a profit.

In fact, to plan properly for cashing out—either to take a break or to start another business—you should recognize this objective before you even start the business. Otherwise, the psychological toll, not to mention the intensity, pressure, time missed with your family, and neglect of your own health, will leave you unprepared and incapable of selling your business for a reasonable price when the time comes.

It may seem contradictory to think about selling your business before you've even started it. In fact, you may not intend to sell your business at all. You may feel satisfied if your company provides you with a reasonable income, and you may not aspire to building a bigger business.

If you aspire to building your business from a tiny acorn of inspiration into a mighty oak of entrepreneurial success, the sooner you start thinking about selling your business, the better the business you'll build.

You have to know when to sell, as well. It makes more sense to sell your business when it's at the peak of its success than when it's descending into a bog of problems, threatened by new technology, lost customers, or more innovative competitors.

You should also know how much your business is worth. A professional business valuator can help you determine this figure. So can an accountant. It's best if you seek this advice before you really need it. Then you won't feel any pressure to overestimate the value of your business. And if you want to add further value, you'll know where you stand now.

The value that you add to your business as you're building it determines the reward that you reap when you sell it. That's why you should start at the outset to focus on the end of the journey. It will inspire you to create the greatest possible value out of your business, not only in enhancing its productivity but in organizing its finances, as well.

A company that provides jobs for its employees, high-quality products or services for its customers, and a return on its investors' money does far more than provide a reward for its founder. It contributes to the economic prosperity of its community, ensures stability, encourages renewal and change, and inspires others to pursue their entrepreneurial dreams. However, if you haven't added value to your company, you may have a hard time selling it for much more than you've invested.

CASHING OUT

Once you decide to sell your company, there are several ways you can choose to do it. These include:

- Selling to employees
- Selling to managers
- Selling to another company
- Selling to another entrepreneur
- Going public

SELLING TO EMPLOYEES

Selling shares in your business to employees can help you achieve several goals in addition to providing you with a return on your investment in your company. An employee stock ownership plan also allows you to reward employees for good performance and to determine a value for the stock in your company without enduring the rigours of a formal public offering.

SELLING TO MANAGERS

Your managers understand your business and could probably run the place themselves. The trouble is, they don't have the cash to buy your share of the business. However, banks, insurance companies, and other financial institutions will provide most of the capital, if your business shows adequate cash flow and healthy assets.

Usually these deals, called Management Buy Outs (MBOs), provide the owner with a small amount of cash up front and the remainder based on a share of the company's profits over a number of years in the future.

However, if your managers make mistakes after they assume control of the company, your share of the profits won't amount to much. Make sure you have sound legal and accounting advice before you embark on an MBO.

SELLING TO ANOTHER COMPANY

Your competitors may be interested in acquiring your business. Presumably, your company has something to offer the other. Your competitor may have more cash; you may have more advanced technology or more creative partnerships with your customers.

In such cases, the entrepreneur usually receives a portion of the selling price initially and a percentage of future profits. Sometimes the entrepreneur ends up working for the newly formed business for a specified period, until the transition is complete.

SELLING TO ANOTHER ENTREPRENEUR

There are many ways to structure the purchase and sale of a company. You can take a combination of cash and shares; you can base your price on a share of future earnings; you can structure a deal that involves a combination of cash, shares, and future earnings.

The least complicated and most advisable way to sell your business is a straight cash deal. That way you're not dependent on the future performance of your business under a new owner.

GOING PUBLIC

As we discussed earlier, taking your company public may sound glamorous and richly rewarding. But it's also a grueling experience that won't necessarily leave you better off than you were when you had a private company.

Apart from the costs and headaches involved in taking a company public, there's a risk that the value of your company's shares will go down rather than up. Meanwhile, there are restrictions on the amount of stock that you and your company's directors can unload on the public at any particular time, so you may have to wait a few years before you start to realize any gains for yourself.

HOW MUCH IS YOUR BUSINESS WORTH?

Here are some general approaches to evaluating a business.

Adjusted Balance-Sheet or Asset Book Value

The price is equivalent to the present value of a company's tangible and intangible assets. The tangible assets of a business might include such things as real estate, lease agreements, customer lists, assumable licences, supplier contracts, prepaid expenses, accounts receivable, furniture, and equipment. Intangible assets include patents, trademarks, and goodwill. Goodwill is the least tangible of all, and the most difficult to evaluate.

Asset Replacement Value

A company may record on its books a value of its assets that doesn't reflect their replacement. You can determine how much it would cost to replace the company's assets to get a truer picture of the company's worth.

Discounted Future Cash Flow

This method is based on the company's future potential. Unfortunately, no one can predict the future with accuracy.

Nevertheless, assuming the business is operating efficiently, it will likely earn money in the future. How much are those earnings worth right now? Determine the company's value and earnings over the next five to ten years. Divide each yearly figure by a number that reflects the risk that the business will not meet these expectations. You add each of these adjusted yearly figures together to obtain your estimate today of the value of future cash flow. (An accountant can help you with this calculation.)

Evaluation of Past Performance

One way to evaluate past performance is to take the company's earnings over the last five years. Factor in the effects of inflation. Calculate the average annual earnings and divide by the capital value. (An accountant can help you with this calculation.)

Comparison

With this method, you compare your business to other businesses in the same industry that have recently been sold.

The drawback to this method is that you might think you're comparing apples to apples when you're really comparing apples to oranges. The other business might have 10 employees over the age of 50; its plant might have sprung a leak in the basement; its owner might have health problems. Before you sell, we strongly urge you to find someone to help you. Like buying a house, buying a business is an emotional experience. A good adviser can keep you on track, keep your emotions from boiling over, and keep you from spending too much money—and buy you a cup of coffee when it's all over.

THE NEXT STAGE

Many entrepreneurs spend so much time building their companies that they have no idea what to do with their money after they sell them. That's why so many entrepreneurs start another business: They can't think of anything better to do.

There are other things in life besides business, however. Here are some ideas to consider if you want to put your cash to good use:

1. Education: From endowing a university professorship to contributing to a high-school program in entrepreneurship, you can make a big difference by supporting an educational institution. Think about the teachers and programs that made a difference in your own life.

2. Culture: A community expresses its soul through the arts. Just as your own business contributed to the economic vitality of your community, the quality of theatres, visual artists, dance groups, orchestras, choirs, operas, and museums enhances the community's cultural vitality and reflects the interest and commitment of the patrons who support them. Sports contribute to a community's cultural life, too. As an entrepreneur with experience in running a business, your money and time are always welcome.

3. New businesses: You have the expertise. You have the experience. Now you have the money. You remember how hard it was for you to build your company, and you probably know how to advise new entrepreneurs about plotting their course as they set out to build their own companies. They don't need just your money. They need you.

THE GRIM ALTERNATIVE: INSOLVENCY AND BANKRUPTCY

Despite their owners' hopes for success, four out of five start-up businesses cease to exist within five years. If it doesn't happen to you, it may happen to a supplier, a customer, or a competitor. The more you know about insolvency, bankruptcy, and receivership, the better prepared you'll be.

INSOLVENCY

Insolvency is a condition that bedevils many companies from time to time. (It even bedevils governments from time to time, so you're in good company.) It happens, in a phrase, when you have too many bills and too few assets to pay them.

A state of insolvency can occur even if your sales are strong and the future of your company looks promising. If several customers decide at the same time that they can't or won't pay you, for example, then you may have trouble scraping together the necessary cash to meet your obligations. If your financial obligations exceed your ability to pay by more than $1,000, your creditors can petition you into bankruptcy.

To resolve the issue, you should communicate with your creditors as soon as you detect a problem with your company's ability to pay its bills. You should talk to your banker and work with your accountant to overcome the obstacle. If you know you're in trouble, the sooner you try to reach an arrangement with your creditors, the better.

An informal proposal by an insolvent business to its creditors usually involves a reduction in the total amount you're obligated to pay them or an amendment to the terms of payment that's more favourable to your business.

You have to present the proposal to each creditor, which can be time-consuming if you do business with dozens of suppliers. To avoid emotional outbursts as you try to swallow your pride, it's usually prudent to present the proposal through a lawyer or receiver.

Given no alternative but a formal proposal, which involves trustee expenses and other costs, creditors will often accept an informal proposal, because they'll receive a higher proportion of the amount you owe them. However, a creditor can also use an informal proposal as grounds for petitioning the business into bankruptcy.

The terms of a formal proposal are governed by the Bankruptcy and Insolvency Act. If the proposal is accepted by a majority of creditors, who represent 75% of the value of the total claims of participating creditors, it becomes binding on all unsecured creditors.

The formal proposal provides an alternative to outright bankruptcy and offers some possibility that creditors will receive at least a portion of the amount owed to them.

The formal proposal must be presented to creditors by a trustee and filed with the Official Receiver. If the creditors reject the proposal, the debtor is deemed to be bankrupt retroactive to the date of proposal.

If the proposal is accepted, the trustee submits it for approval to the court and distributes proceeds to creditors under terms of the proposal. Preferred creditors include the government for employee tax deductions, employees with wages outstanding, and certain others.

If the debtor complies with the terms of the proposal, he carries on with his business. If he doesn't, he's automatically bankrupt.

Secured creditors are not bound by a proposal under the Bankruptcy and Insolvency Act. However, a formal proposal must provide for payment of secured creditors and full payment of trustee's fees and expenses.

There are several variations of the formal proposal, and you can create your own depending on your circumstances and the preferences of your creditors. The options range from providing creditors with a percentage of your company's profits to extending the time over which you must pay your creditors.

BANKRUPTCY

Behind most successful businesses lies at least one failure. Many of the entrepreneurs who start a business have come close to or experienced bankruptcy once in their lives. Bankruptcy is a critical and necessary element in our daily commercial lives. Without it, companies that go out of business would never be able to start another business.

Once a company goes bankrupt and its assets are distributed to creditors, the owner can proceed unburdened with excessive debts that otherwise would haunt him for the rest of his life. Bankruptcy proceedings also allow at least some creditors to eke out a pittance from the bankrupt company.

In a bankruptcy proceeding, a trustee, acting on behalf of the creditors, tries to squeeze as much cash out of the bankrupt company's remaining assets as he can, then distributes the money to creditors in proportion to the amounts owed.

The trustee is appointed by the Official Receiver, who works for the Superintendent of Bankruptcy, who works for the federal government. The trustee is usually a chartered accountant licensed by the government to divide the assets of bankrupt companies and distribute them to creditors.

The trustee can't touch any assets of the bankrupt company that have been pledged to secure a debt. These assets are the property of the secured creditors.

Another type of creditor is the preferred creditor, who ranks behind the secured creditors but in front of the unsecured creditors. Preferred creditors include governments, employees with wages owing, and the Workers Compensation Board.

Finally come the unsecured creditors who receive what's owed to them only after the secured and preferred creditors have been paid.

BANKRUPTCY INFORMATION

You can get more information on bankruptcy from Consumer and Corporate Affairs Canada, listed in the Blue Pages of your phone book.

You can declare yourself bankrupt by assigning all your property to a trustee and your company can do the same. The trustee then turns the assets into cash and distributes it to your creditors. If you have personally guaranteed a loan you will not walk away easily.

IF YOU'RE A CREDITOR

If you're a creditor of a company in bankruptcy, you'll want to know that the trustee has access to as many of the company's assets as possible and that the owner of the bankrupt company hasn't fraudulently cashed in his assets before declaring bankruptcy. The trustee examines all transactions involving the bankrupt company that have occurred within the last year.

You'll also have to verify your own claim against the debtor, with an invoice or a promissory note. You'll have to attend a meeting of creditors, usually within three weeks of the trustee's appointment.

Under the supervision of the trustee, the bankrupt company has to relinquish all its remaining assets and open its books to the public. If the owner tries to circumvent the terms of the Bankruptcy and Insolvency Act, he can wind up in jail or incur a stiff fine.

WHEN BANKRUPTCIES OCCUR
More firms close their doors in their 10th year than at any other stage of their existence, according to a study by Dun & Bradstreet Canada.

In the case of an individual, the trustee must apply to the court within one year of bankruptcy for a discharge from bankruptcy on behalf of the debtor. The court will either grant an absolute discharge or issue a conditional discharge, under which the bankrupt debtor must meet further conditions, such as paying his creditors an additional $50,000, before an absolute discharge takes effect.

RECEIVERSHIP

If a corporation can't comply with the terms of a debenture or security—issued by agreement as security for a loan—then the secured lender can appoint a receiver to assume control of the debtor's assets. The receiver can manage the business until the business or its assets are sold. Or he can give the debtor an opportunity to refinance.

A receiver operates under the tenets of commercial law rather than the Bankruptcy and Insolvency Act, although he is required to file certain notices under the Act.

SUCCESSION PLANNING

Rooted in the here and now, most entrepreneurs regard the concept of succession as an alien thought, like making a will. It's something you consider in your spare moments, when all the millions of other details involved in running a business have been put to rest.

Yet as entrepreneurs like the McCains, Eatons, Irvings, Woodwards, Belzbergs, Thomsons, Bronfmans, Stronachs and hundreds of less notorious families throughout Canada have discovered, the earlier you address the issue of succession, the easier the transition will be when the time comes.

In a survey by Korn/Ferry International, an executive search firm based in New York, almost 70% of corporate boards said that succession was second in importance only to survival. But as CEO Richard Ferry observes, while 81% of outside directors ranked succession as the most important board priority, only 36% of board chairs ranked it among the top three priorities.

In the process, you might save yourself from decades of animosity; save your sons and daughters from descending into a family feud; save hundreds of thousands of dollars in legal fees; and perhaps save your company itself for another generation.

Management succession and ownership succession are two different issues. Sometimes owners also manage the business; but in many cases, the owners hire professional managers. Taking your company public can help to ease the transition in ownership from one generation to the next and reassure management that their jobs won't be in jeopardy if anything should happen to the founder.

Ownership comes with its own set of requirements, and it helps if people are prepared for them. It involves concerns like how you'll handle cousins joining the company; will all the kids receive equal incomes or will they be paid according to their jobs; how will they settle decisions about buying and selling their share of the company, and so on.

Of course, succession is just one of many issues that preoccupy the leaders of small firms. While they're wrestling with more immediate problems like increasing sales, improving quality, and meeting next Thursday's payroll, they don't have much time to spend wondering about who might replace them. The few thoughts they do have about succession usually remain tightly locked in their own heads. Without a formal plan, the transition from one leader to the next can disrupt routines and threaten the existence of the firm.

It can be especially disruptive in firms run by their founders, which have yet to experience a change in leadership. "An organization that has experienced the exit of its first president is almost 100 times more likely to fail in the year following the succession than a comparable organization that has had stable executive leadership," writes Heather Haveman of Duke University.

In fact, Haveman maintains, succession has a more profound effect on growing companies than on companies that are stable or shrinking. "Rapidly growing organizations get into trouble and are less likely to survive [succession] than shrinking or stable organizations," she says in her study, published in the *Academy of Management Journal.*

The leader of a small, growing company may worry about succession when he's not worrying about finances, deadlines, and expansion. Besides, why worry about succession when you can't find enough good people to work for you in the first place?

"In companies suffering from growth," says James Carlisle of consultants Ernst & Young, "there's a whole layer of management that's missing, and the company doesn't have the time to develop them internally. So while they're looking outside the company for managers, they put people into slots that they're not capable of filling."

A PLAN THAT WORKS
Some companies have found ways to handle the process of succession. They not only manage to identify potential successors, they manage to keep them employed with the company as well. In most cases, the companies offer some form of equity ownership to potential leaders. Meanwhile, they present them with new challenges and expanding responsibilities.

Vickers & Benson Advertising Ltd. in Toronto has survived four rituals of succession in its 70-year history. "We've always had succession planning," says Terry O'Malley, a Harvard graduate who rose to the position of Chairman and Executive Creative Director at the firm. (He is now Partner and Creative Adviser.)

In the process of succession at the privately held company, its leaders first identify the individuals who have what it takes to assume control of the firm. Then they help the next generation acquire an equity interest in the firm. "The people we'd like to see participate in the company's succession are usually in their 30s and 40s. They have kids and a mortgage. At that stage of their careers, to become shareholders in the company presents a formidable obstacle. So we have a system that allows them to build their equity slowly."

Potential successors may not share the same attributes as the founder of a business. The qualities of stubborn tenacity, ruthless drive, and focused intensity that motivate an entrepreneur to build a company can become a liability in the leader of an established firm. Who wants to work for someone who thinks job descriptions are for lard-butted sissies or discuss a deal over lunch with someone who can't stop tapping the water glass with his pen because he's too preoccupied with his own agenda?

"Individuals with the entrepreneurial skills to establish and grow a firm are fundamentally different in many ways from those who can effectively manage larger, more bureaucratic firms," observe Robert Drazin and Robert Kazanjian of Emory Business School in Atlanta. "As ventures grow and mature over time, different functional skills are required."

A GUIDE TO SUCCESSION

According to UK consultant Peter Wallum, a contributor to *Personnel Management* magazine, the strategic processes of succession management are:

1. Analysis of the demand for managers and professionals by level, function and skill;

2. Audit of existing executives and projection of likely future supply from internal and external sources;

3. Planning individual career paths based on objective estimates of future needs and drawing on reliable performance appraisals and assessments of potential;

4. Career counselling undertaken in the context of a realistic understanding of the future needs of the firm, as well as those of the individual;

5. Accelerated promotion schemes with development targeted against the future needs of the business;

6. Performance-related training and development to prepare individuals for future roles as well as their current responsibilities;

7. Planned strategic recruitment not only to fill short-term needs but also to provide people for development to meet future needs;

8. The actual processes by which appointments are filled.

big money ideas

11

Over the last 10 chapters we've tried to show you how entrepreneurs think, and to give you some tools and information about personal and business planning. We've discussed the use of advisers and indicated how you can harvest the fruits of your efforts. Now we'll provide a synopsis of the big money ideas that many successful entrepreneurs have used to achieve their dreams.

1. Big money comes from aligning your personal goals with those of your business and your customers.

Here are two small cases to illustrate this point:

- Elaine and Susan worked for a market research firm that was owned by a large advertising agency. The agency decided to sell the research firm. Each of the women examined her personal needs and goals and discovered that, with minor exceptions, both were looking for independence from corporate politics, an opportunity to define and control her own future, financial independence (defined as $150,000 a year in salary and a good retirement), more time with her family, and a desire to build something for herself.

  After comparing their goals Elaine and Susan decided to start their own research firm. They worked well together as a team and, over a period of five years, they built their business to the point that each partner was making over $200,000 a year, and their retirement was guaranteed.

This is a good example of personal goals aligning with business goals to produce the desired financial results.

- Carl and Steve weren't so fortunate. The two men worked for a market research firm owned by a major advertising agency. The agency decided to sell the research firm. Each man was upset that he didn't get the promotion he'd expected.

  Rather than proving themselves once again to the new owners, they decided to start their own market research firm. Within a year the firm failed, and each partner blamed the other for the failure. In fact both are to blame. Had they looked at their own personal goals they would have discovered that one partner wanted to make as much money as possible to keep up with other members of his spouse's family, and he didn't care about spending time with his family. The other partner wanted to prove that he could produce high-quality work. He was driven to produce the best research no matter what the costs, but he worked only 35 hours a week, spending his remaining time with his large and extensive family. Meanwhile, he needed only a small income to survive. In short, Carl and Steve did not share common goals.

This is a good illustration of a partnership doomed to failure from the beginning. The partners' personal and business goals did not align.

We have only 168 hours in a week. After allowing for sleeping and eating, we're left with about 80 hours a week for family, work, and recreation. How we choose to spend these hours will determine our success, measured by how close we come to achieving our personal goals.

2. Big money minimizes risk.

All entrepreneurs share an aversion to risk. They believe in being innovative and moving forward by taking small steps along a path where the risk is clearly defined and acceptable to them. They can walk away at any time, perhaps not gladly, but at least knowing the price that they'll pay.

Starting a new business is always risky. By defining how much money you're prepared to put into the new business at the beginning you've effectively defined what you're prepared to lose while measuring the potential up side.

Here's an example:

- Leonard works in the food industry. He decides that he wants to buy a franchise operation that will cost him $50,000 in fees and another $50,000 in working capital. He has reviewed his personal financial situation and has a net worth of $350,000. He decides he will risk one-third of his accumulated wealth on this venture.

    Leonard begins by meeting the franchisor to get more information. He then speaks to a number of current franchisees to understand the pluses and minuses of working with this franchisor. He knows that, if he concludes that this franchise is not a good investment or will not allow him to reach his goals, he can stop the process at any point, losing only his investment to date—in this case, some of his time and perhaps a minor deposit with the franchisor.

    All successful small business owners follow a similar conservative step-by-step approach. They measure risk and understand the down side, then move forward.

3. Big money arranges its affairs to have money available from a variety of sources.

Small business owners tend to use their personal resources as a source of financing for their business. With minor exceptions, this guarantees that they will not achieve their goals. To succeed, you should divide your personal finances into four categories:

- short-term money (also called "if the world comes to an end")
- real estate
- tax-sheltered funds, and
- other investments.

When you begin to execute your plan, you start by ensuring that you have enough short-term savings to support you, after taxes, for about four months. For example, if you need $4,000 a month after taxes to pay your usual bills, you should have short-term savings of about $16,000 before you start to execute your plan. If you get sick or encounter other problems, you can still pay your bills for at least four months without worrying. Next you want to pay down as much as possible of your mortgage for your principal residence. Your mortgage interest is not tax-deductible, so the faster you pay off the loan, the better. Putting money away in tax-sheltered funds for your retirement is critical. By definition, entrepreneurs rely on no one else but themselves to pay for their retirement. The government-funded Canada Pension Plan will simply not be adequate for your retirement. By making your maximum RRSP contribution, you can accumulate tax-free a significant amount of money by the time you retire. If you don't have enough money to pay down your mortgage and contribute to an RRSP, you should examine your situation carefully. Under most circumstances, you would be best advised to pay off your mortgage first. However, under some circumstances, you may be better off financially if you take a longer-term fixed mortgage for, say, ten years, which will fix your monthly payments, and then make your maximum RRSP contribution each year.

After taking care of all these needs, smart money will then start to accumulate investments in other vehicles. These may include mutual funds, antiques, a cottage, etc. Once you reach this stage you should consult a professional money manager.

Here's an example:

- Tom earned $100,000 from his business. He paid taxes of about $40,000 and needed $3,000 a month to live, including a monthly mortgage payment of $1,000. His mortgage of $150,000 was due for renewal in three years. He was eligible to make his maximum RRSP contribution each year.

   To execute an appropriate financial strategy, Tom needs to accumulate about $12,000 in short-term savings and keep another $12,000 available to contribute to his RRSP. To maximize his RRSP contribution to $13,500, he should, if necessary, borrow the additional $1,500 and repay it from his tax refund. Next year he will be in a position to put the maximum contribution to his RRSP, with about $6,500 left over for longer-term savings. By the time his mortgage comes up for renewal he will have about $13,000 available to make a lump-sum payment. This will reduce his monthly payments significantly and allow him to save more. Tom plans to retire in about 20 years. By following this plan he can accumulate a significant amount over that period.

4. Big money has a harvest plan.

It may sound silly, but you shouldn't start a business unless you know how you'll get out of it. Small business owners commonly start a business and watch it grow to a point where it pays the bills but leaves little left over to reward them for their hard work. In such a situation, you're trapped. If you tried to sell it, the business wouldn't be worth much. Who wants a business that only pays the bills? Nor can you walk away from it, because you don't have the money to pay your bills indefinitely. You'll be stuck with this business for a long time.

Smart businesspeople have a harvest plan before they begin. This plan provides a way to leave a marginal or losing business and identifies a time to harvest the rewards of a successful business.

Here's an example:

- For over ten years Sally has run a public relations firm, which has become very successful. On her 55th birthday she plans to sell the business and move on. She is now 47. She has consulted with her family and her chartered accountant about her plan. Her family is supportive, which boosts her confidence. Her accountant, meanwhile, has pointed out ways in which she could sell her business to maximize her return. More important, her accountant has suggested ways that she can achieve her goal.

  Following her accountant's advice, she increased the value of her firm over a few years from $200,000 to more than $750,000. When she was 53 an advertising agency that she dealt with offered to buy her firm. She got a maximum price and a three-year contract to continue to run the firm, along with a significant salary and bonus package. When she left the advertising agency at age 55, she had over $1 million in the bank just from the sale of her business.

5. Big money keeps assets offshore.

Canada is an export nation. We export many of our goods and services to foreign countries. Smart money will look at the opportunity of setting up a business in a low-tax foreign jurisdiction. This business must be an active one, not simply a company set up offshore to handle passive investments. An active offshore business isn't taxable in Canada (although it's subject to tax in the offshore country), whereas a passive operation is taxable in Canada no matter where the investments are held. Examine your business and determine if you have a lot of revenue from offshore. This might justify a separate active business in that country. At a lower tax rate the wealth accumulation can be enormous. However, you should never take such a step without seeking expert advice.

Here's an example:

- Mary ran a company that manufactured tires, which she sold in about ten countries. Mary had reached a stage in her financial affairs where she was earning enough salary from her company to live comfortably in Canada while accumulating her maximum tax-free investments. After consulting with her chartered accountant she decided to open a company in the United States. This company actively sold her company's tires within the United States and also handled most international sales. The tires were manufactured in Canada and sold at a small profit (by coincidence the profit always maximized the use of the Canadian manufacturing special tax rates) to the U.S. company.

  The U.S. company was quite successful. It also paid tax at a significantly lower rate than the Canadian company. The difference was left in the United States to assist with the growth of the company. When Mary retired with careful planning she was able to sell her company for a much higher price than she'd expected.

6. Big money incudes the whole family in the plan and splits income.

Family members who are performing actual work for your business can receive compensation. Business owners commonly pay their spouses for work performed, for example. However, many small business owners forget to pay their children for their work. In order to satisfy Revenue Canada the work must be legitimate, the rate of pay must be comparable to the rate you'd pay a non-family member, and it must be within the capabilities of the child to perform. The family members should have social insurance numbers, receive T4s, and have proper withholding tax taken off and remitted.

Here's an example:

- Marion has been married to Peter for almost 25 years. They have three children, ages 19, 16, and 12. Marion runs a direct mail business. She often needs to stuff envelopes, print letters, etc. Marion makes about $140,000 per year. Until recently,

Peter worked as a clerk and made about $40,000 per year. Their children held part-time jobs.

Last year Marion hired her husband part-time to assist with the operation of her business, paying him about $35,000. She also hired her eldest child to do some computer work, paying her about $8,000 a year. Her second-eldest child did some manual labour for Marion's company and earned about $5,000 a year. Her youngest child earned about $2,000 stuffing envelopes.

By shifting her income among her family in a bona fide manner, Marion accomplished the following:

- Her husband now qualified for his maximum RRSP contribution.
- Her eldest child earned enough to pay for her university tuition and some expenses.
- Her middle and youngest children earned enough to pay for their yearly allowances.
- The payments were all tax deductible within the firm.
- The income to her children was essentially not taxable.
- And her children became eligible to contribute to an RRSP.

7. Big money keeps it simple.

Successful individuals from all walks of life keep their lives simple. They do this in part by being well-organized about their personal affairs. Peace of mind minimizes stress and maximizes financial returns.

Here's an example:

- Jane, the owner of a stationery wholesaler, heard from a friend about an opportunity to save some money on her automobile insurance. She called immediately and was told that the company wanted a copy of her current policy before quoting on this new opportunity. She remembered putting her insurance policy in a safe place but wasn't sure where. She left the office and returned home, where she spent about an hour looking for her policy, but to no avail. She called her current broker and asked him to fax a copy to her. Her broker said he would gladly drop one off as he wanted to see her anyway. They met the next day for an hour while her broker tried to increase her coverage at a higher premium. Finally, she sent a copy of her policy to the new insurer. The company sent a quote a few days later that would save Jane about 10%. Jane was pleased.

However, her sales manager then told her that he had tried to reach her over the previous few days to accompany him on a call to a current client who was unhappy about the quality of stationery he was receiving. Jane had been at home searching for her insurance policy at the time. The sales manager had rescheduled the meeting, but the next time he tried to reach Jane she was meeting her insurance broker and couldn't be disturbed. The client decided to take his business to another supplier. Jane saved 10% on her car insurance but lost a long-term customer, simply because she didn't organize her life to keep it simple and herself free to focus on the important issues.

8. Big money uses expert advice.

Astute entrepreneurs know they don't have time to grow and manage their business and still do all the research necessary to invest their money wisely. Instead, they hire professional money managers to do this for them. A good money manager will ask for your personal financial goals before suggesting where to invest your hard-earned money.

It's a good idea to diversify your financial management among a number of money managers. For example, if you have $200,000 to manage, give $100,000 to each of two managers, then measure their performance on a regular basis.

Here's an example:

*   Bill knew he was too busy to take care of his money himself. He had accumulated about $130,000 over a number of years, but he did not keep a close eye on how the money was performing and growing. He was shocked to discover that, after two years, his investments were now worth only $110,000.

    Bill asked his friends for the names of their investment advisers. He met each of them and chose one to help him. He also made a point of checking the status of his investments each quarter. He was also pleased that his new adviser called at the end of each quarter to update him on the status of his investments. Over the year, he earned a 15% return on his capital.

9. Big money plans clearly.

All successful entrepreneurs take the time to plan. Starting with your vision for the firm, a written business plan articulates all the necessary elements to ensure the success of your business. If you have trouble putting your plan on paper it usually means that you haven't thought enough about it. Without clarity, you generally will not succeed. A business plan is your most important big money tool.

10. Big money obtains different financing at different times.

Money is the fuel for business growth and success. Winning entrepreneurs take the time to ensure that they have adequate amounts of money for their needs. The best time to get more money is when you don't need it. In good times, increase your line of credit, sell equity and, in general, raise more money. This will help your business succeed.

There are many different sources of financing available. Smart entrepreneurs hire strong financial advisers to keep them abreast of the latest trends and in touch with the key players in the money markets.

11. Big money runs a tight ship.

Running a tight operation will save you a great deal of money. Money sticks to well-organized businesses and pours out of loosely run businesses. By staying on top of the details and relying on good people to help you, you can keep your firm well organized and performing strongly.

Many small businesses prefer not to have a Board of Directors, for example, so they use an advisory board instead. The advantages of an advisory board are that you can more easily add or delete members, and that members of an advisory board, unlike directors, incur no personal liability in their board-related activities.

12. Big money plans for the future.

Smart business owners take the time to plan their affairs for their retirement or death. Through sound planning, you can deal with the issues related to sibling rivalry, for example, taxes, and the continuation of the family name. Since close to 50% of all marriages end in divorce, for example, your spouse could end up controlling your business and assets if you don't set up your estate properly. There are many different ways to set up an estate plan. Start by determining exactly what you'd like to happen.

Here's an example:

- Cybill and Robert have been married for 20 years. They operate a manufacturing company. They have three children age 19, 21, and 23. They're concerned about the amount of tax they'll have to pay on their capital gain when they retire. They decide to set up a trust, naming as beneficiaries their three children. They transfer ownership in the manufacturing company to the trust. This freezes the amount of capital gain that they've made on the shares and transfers any new gain to the trust, to be taxed at some point in the hands of the beneficiaries. They then assume the role of trustee, thereby continuing to control the company. Should one of their children divorce, the value of the trust is not considered part of the marriage settlement.

FINAL WORD

No one will take care of your success except yourself. Start your successful planning program by understanding your personal vision. Then get your personal financial plan in order, develop a clear business plan, hire good advisers, and plan how you'll harvest the results of all your hard work. Now it's up to you.

bibliography

BOOKS

Budd, John et al. *Canadian Guide to Personal Financial Management.* Toronto: Prentice Hall Canada Inc., 1996.

Bygrave, William D. *The Portable MBA in Entrepreneurship.* New York: John Wiley & Sons Inc., 1994.

Ginsberg, Laurence and McDougall, Bruce. *The Complete Idiot's Guide to Being an Entrepreneur in Canada.* Toronto: Prentice Hall Canada Inc.,1996.

Gumpert, David E. (ed.). *Growing Concerns: Building and Managing the Smaller Business.* New York: John Wiley & Sons Inc., 1984.

Hiam, Alexander W., and Olander, Karen W. *The Entrepreneur's Complete Sourcebook.* New York: Prentice Hall Inc., 1996.

McDougall, Bruce and Reardon, Michael. *The Complete Idiot's Guide to Personal Finance for Canadians.* Toronto: Prentice Hall Canada Inc.,1994.

ARTICLES

Bhide, Amar. "The Questions Every Entrepreneur Must Answer." *Harvard Business Review*, November-December 1996, 120-130.

Sahlman, William A. "How to write a great business plan." *Harvard Business Review*, July-August 1997, 98-109.

appendix 1

These sites on the World Wide Web may be useful to you.

Site Name	Site Address	Site Features
Quick Advice Inc.	www.quickadvice.com	Small Business online advice
Quicken	www.quicken.ca	In-depth resource site
Bank of Montreal	www.bmo.com	Numerous calculators (Rent vs. Own, How much can I afford?, Mortgage number cruncher, mortgage insurance, blend extend, 15 + 15, decision maker, investment, future vs. present, budget for students) investment indicator game, retirement income estimator
Royal Bank	www.royalbank.com	Stock calculator for commission for buy/sell
Scotiabank	www.scotiabank.ca	RRSP Catch-up loan calculator
Toronto Dominion Bank	www.tdbank.ca	WebBroker, MicroMax, TeleMax, TD Access PC Broker (online PC banking brokerage service)
CIBC	www.cibc.com	SAM—your Strategic Asset Manager
mbanx	www.mbanx.com	Banking online 24 hours a day, 365 days a year
State Farm Insurance	www.statefarm.com	Has mortgage and loan calculator, retirement calculator, savings calculator
Allstate Insurance	www.allstate.com	Auto, Home Planning, Life & Estate Planning Calculators and Tools
London Life	www.londonlife.com	Manage your retirement
Prudential	www.prudential.com	Retirement planning, insurance, investing, banking services, estate planning, education funding, health care, real estate, business services

appendix 2
personal financial planner

(blank forms)

This appendix contains blank forms to determine where you are today. Many financial planners will use similar forms. These are copies of our firm's forms for your use.

Full Legal Name

_____

Date this planner completed

While financial planning is a continuous process it is useful to look at your situation at a point in time in light of your financial goals and adjust your plans as you go. This booklet provides a snapshot of your financial situation at the date noted above. This information is geared to provide you and your professional advisor(s) with all relevant details to highlight areas requiring further planning. In analyzing this information, it will be necessary to make certain assumptions with which to perform your analysis. This is an ongoing process to be revised annually or as your circumstances change.

Every individual's situation is different. Be certain to include considerations that you feel are relevant but that are not listed in this planner.

The Financial Planning Process begins with the following:

(1)   Your completion of this questionnaire. This may require a couple of hours depending upon the state of your financial records.

(2)   A meeting with you (and perhaps your spouse), with a copy of your latest tax return(s).

Financial Planner
Basic Information

		YOU	SPOUSE/ SIGNIFICANT OTHER
1.0	Name (Surname, Given)		
1.1	Home Address		
1.2	Telephone (Business)	( )	( )
	(Residence)	( )	( )
	(Fax)	( )	( )
1.3	Marital Status	Single__ Married__ Divorced__ Common Law__	Single__ Married__ Divorced__ Common Law__
1.4	Date of Birth		
1.5	Citizenship	Canadian____ or ____	Canadian____ or ____
1.6	Children	Name Date of Birth	Same as Spouse____ or Add
1.7	Employer Name		
1.8	Employer Address		
1.9	Type of Work		

Financial Planner
Permanent Record

	YOU	SPOUSE/ SIGNIFICANT OTHER
2.0 Do you have a will?	Yes___ No___	Yes___ No___
2.1 If yes, date of will		
and location held		
2.2 Powers of Attorney signed	Yes___ No___	Yes___ No___
2.3 Name of solicitor		
Address of solicitor		
Phone number of solicitor		
2.4 Marriage contract	Yes___ No___	Yes___ No___
2.5 Separation agreement	Yes___ No___	Yes___ No___
2.6 Divorce agreement	Yes___ No___	Yes___ No___
2.7 Name of insurance agent		
Phone # of insurance agent		

Financial Planner
Objectives and Special Considerations

3.0 OBJECTIVES

Describe your three major financial objectives, giving consideration to:
- Providing financial security for your family
- Reducing your income taxes
- Increasing the return on your investment assets
- Saving for major expenditures such as buying a home
- Saving for retirement or other long-term goals

	YOU	SPOUSE
1		
2		
3		

SPECIAL CONSIDERATIONS

3.1 Do any of your relatives require special financial assistance (i.e. physically or mentally challenged, elderly, poor)?

WHO?	ASSISTANCE REQUIRED?

Financial Planner
You and Your Spouse's Personal Balance Sheet

	TYPE/TERM/ CONDITIONS (OR LIST)	APPROX. RATE OF RETURN	MARKET VALUE AS OF PLANNING DATE		
			YOU	SPOUSE	COMBINED
ASSETS					
Short-term Investments					
Cash in Bank					
Savings Accounts					
Canada Savings Bonds					
Treasury Bills					
Money Market Funds					
Sub-total					
Medium-term Investments					
(e.g. GIC, Stripped	(1,2,3,4,5 year, Fed, Prov,				
Coupons, Bonds,	type of Mutual Fund)				
Stocks, Mutual Funds)					
Sub-total					
Employee Savings Plans					
Sub-total					
Long-term Investments					
D.P.S.P.'s					
R.R.S.P.'s (GIC's, T-bills,					
Bonds, Mutual Funds)					
Pension Plan Value					
Sub-total					

Financial Planner
You and Your Spouse's Personal Balance Sheet (Cont'd)

	TYPE/TERM/ CONDITIONS (OR LIST)	APPROX. RATE OF RETURN	MARKET VALUE AS OF PLANNING DATE		
			YOU	SPOUSE	COMBINED
PERSONAL ASSETS					
Home					
Cottage					
Cars					
Jewellery					
Art					
Sub-total					
BUSINESS ASSETS					
Shares in small business					
Value of sole proprietorship or partnership					
Sub-total					
OTHER					
Limited partnerships					
Rental properties					
Sub-total					
TOTAL ASSETS					

Financial Planner
You and Your Spouse's Personal Balance Sheet (Cont'd)

	TYPE/TERM/ CONDITIONS (OR LIST)	APPROX. RATE OF RETURN	MARKET VALUE AS OF PLANNING DATE		
			YOU	SPOUSE	COMBINED
LIABILITIES (What you owe)					
Credit card debt					
—VISA					
—MASTERCARD					
—Other					
Lines of Credit					
Personal Loans					
Car Loans					
Mortgage—Term, Expiry,					
Interest rate,					
Amortization,					
Principal outstanding					
Other—					
TOTAL LIABILITIES					
NET WORTH (Total Assets — Total Liabilities)					

Financial Planner
Sources of Income

	YOU	SPOUSE	COMBINED
From Employment			
Basic salary/year			
Average bonus/year			
Taxable benefit details			
Self-employment Income			
Interest			
Dividends			
Capital gains			
Rental income			
Limited partnership income			
Other Income			
TOTAL INCOME			

Financial Planner
Sources of Expenditure

	YOU	SPOUSE	COMBINED

SHELTER
- Mortgage payment or rent
- Property Taxes
- Insurance
- Utilities (light, heat, water)
- Maintenance
- Gardener Upkeep
- Other—(incl. cable)

Sub-total

FOOD, HOUSEHOLD, ETC.
- Food
- Household
- Telephone
- Personal Care (hair, makeup)
- Clothing
- Other—

Sub-total

TRANSPORTATION
- Car Payments
- Insurance
- Gasoline
- Maintenance
- Public Transportation
- Other—

Sub-total

Financial Planner
Sources of Expenditure (Cont'd)

	YOU	SPOUSE	COMBINED
FINANCING			
Credit Card Payments (if balance outstanding)			
Loan Payment			
–			
–			
–			
DISCRETIONARY			
Entertainment			
Dining Out			
Gifts			
Fees, Books, Etc.			
Club Dues			
Other–			
Sub-total			
MISCELLANEOUS			
Medical/Dental Expenses			
Life & Disability Insurance Premiums			
Payroll Deductions Other Than Income Tax			
Other–			
Sub-total			
OTHER ITEMS			
Renovations planned			
Vacations			
Other Plans			
TOTAL BASIC LIFESTYLE EXPENDITURES			

Financial Planner
Schedule of Insurance

LIFE INSURANCE	YOU	SPOUSE
From Employer		
Life Coverage		
Type of Plan		
Insurance Company		
Cash Value (if any)		
Private Insurance		
Life Coverage		
Type of Plan		
Insurance Company		
Cash Value (if any)		
DISABILITY INSURANCE		
From Employer		
Amount paid per month		
Private		
Amount paid per month		

appendix 3
personal financial plan

Jane Jones and Bill Smith are married. Jane owns her own manufacturing business, and Bill works for a company that has been having some financial difficulty.

This five-year plan is to give you a feel for how a plan might be put together. As mentioned in Appendix 1, there are a number of tools available on the Web to assist you in preparing your plan.

Jane and Bill discussed their personal goals together and agreed on the following:

1. Financial independence by age 55. Financial independence means having enough money to live their normal lives without having to work. Estimated at $3,000,000 net worth excluding real estate.

2. Grow Jane's business to the point where Bill can quit his job and work in the business full time.

3. Have enough money to take care of Bill's mother.

They would review these objectives each year on New Years day.

Jane Jones and Bill Smith
Personal Financial Plan

JANE JONES–INCOME	1997	1998	1999	2000	2001	2002
Employment income	100,000	100,000	100,000	100,000	100,000	100,000
Bonus/taxable benefits/self-empl inc						
Dividends	5,000	5,100	5,202	5,306	5,412	5,520
Interest & investment income	7,500	8,250	9,075	9,983	10,981	12,079
Limited Partnership income	8,000	8,000	8,000	8,000	8,000	8,000
Taxable capital gains	1,500	3,650	7,723	9,711	10,607	11,401
Sub-total	122,000	125,000	130,000	133,000	135,000	137,000
RPP deduction						
RRSP deduction	(13,500)	(13,500)	(13,500)	(13,500)	(13,500)	(13,500)
Interest expenses	0	0	0	0	0	0
Net cap losses from other yrs	0	0	0	0	0	0
Capital gains deduction	0	0	0	0	0	0
Social benefits repayment	0	0	0	0	0	0
Taxable income	108,500	111,500	116,500	119,500	121,500	123,500
Personal taxes–est	(45,049)	(46,645)	(49,305)	(50,901)	(51,965)	(53,029)
NET CASH TO JANE	**63,451**	**64,855**	**67,195**	**68,599**	**69,535**	**70,471**

BILL SMITH—INCOME	1997	1998	1999	2000	2001	2002
Employment income	75,000	76,500	78,030	79,591	81,182	82,806
Self Employment income	25,000	26,250	27,562	28,941	30,388	31,907
Dividends						
Interest & investment income	7,000	7,700	8,470	9,317	10,249	11,274
Limited Partnership income						
Taxable capital gains						
Sub-total	107,000	110,450	114,062	117,849	121,819	125,987
RPP deduction						
RRSP deduction	(13,500)	(13,500)	(13,500)	(13,500)	(13,500)	(13,500)
Interest expenses						
Capital losses						
Capital gains deduction						
Social benefits repayment						
Professional dues						
Child care expenses						
Taxable income	93,500	96,950	100,562	104,349	108,319	112,487
Personal taxes	(37,069)	(38,904)	(40,826)	(42,840)	(44,953)	(47,170)
NET CASH TO BILL	**56,431**	**58,046**	**59,736**	**61,509**	**63,366**	**65,317**

COMBINED INCOME

	1997	1998	1999	2000	2001	2002
Employment income	175,000	176,500	178,030	179,591	181,182	182,806
Self employ't or other employ't income	25,000	26,250	27,562	28,941	30,388	31,907
Dividends	5,000	5,100	5,202	5,306	5,412	5,520
Interest & investment income	14,500	15,950	17,545	19,300	21,229	23,352
Limited Partnership income	8,000	8,000	8,000	8,000	8,000	8,000
Taxable capital gains	1,500	3,650	7,723	9,711	10,607	11,401
Total Income	229,000	235,450	244,062	250,849	256,818	262,986
RPP deduction	0	0	0	0	0	0
RRSP deduction	(27,000)	(27,000)	(27,000)	(27,000)	(27,000)	(27,000)
Interest expenses	0	0	0	0	0	0
Capital losses	0	0	0	0	0	0
Capital gains deduction	0	0	0	0	0	0
Social benefits repayment	0	0	0	0	0	0
Child care expenses	0	0	0	0	0	0
Taxable income	202,000	208,450	217,062	223,849	229,818	235,986
Personal taxes	(82,118)	(85,549)	(90,131)	(93,741)	(96,917)	(100,199)
NET CASH COMBINED	**119,882**	**122,901**	**126,931**	**130,108**	**132,901**	**135,787**

COMBINED EXPENDITURES	1997	1998	1999	2000	2001	2002
NET CASH GENERATED	119,882	122,901	126,931	130,107	132,901	135,788
COMBINED EXPENDITURES						
Property taxes	5,000	5,100	5,202	5,306	5,412	5,520
House insurance	2,000	2,040	2,081	2,122	2,165	2,208
Utilities	8,000	8,160	8,323	8,490	8,659	8,833
Maintenance	5,000	5,100	5,202	5,306	5,412	5,520
Gardener upkeep/winter	300	306	312	318	325	331
Other (cable etc.)	1,000	1,020	1,040	1,061	1,082	1,104
Food	12,000	12,240	12,485	12,734	12,989	13,249
Household	12,000	12,240	12,485	12,734	12,989	13,249
Telephone	1,000	1,020	1,040	1,061	1,082	1,104
Personal care	2,000	2,040	2,081	2,122	2,165	2,208
Clothing	10,000	10,200	10,404	10,612	10,824	11,041
Other—misc	5,000	5,100	5,202	5,306	5,412	5,520
Public Transportation	200	204	208	212	216	221
Gas	1,500	1,530	1,561	1,592	1,624	1,656
Entertainment	1,000	1,020	1,040	1,061	1,082	1,104
Eating Out	1,000	1,020	1,040	1,061	1,082	1,104
Gifts	2,000	2,040	2,081	2,122	2,165	2,208
Club dues	2,000	2,040	2,081	2,122	2,165	2,208
School fees/Camp	5,000	5,100	5,202	5,306	5,412	5,520
Medical/Dental/Pets	7,000	7,140	7,283	7,428	7,577	7,729
Renovations planned	5,000	5,100	5,202	5,306	5,412	5,520
Vacations	10,000	10,200	10,404	10,612	10,824	11,041
Misc.	2,000	2,040	2,081	2,122	2,165	2,208
TOTAL EXPENDITURES	100,000	102,000	104,040	106,116	108,240	110,406
AVAILABLE FOR SAVINGS	19,882	20,901	22,891	23,991	24,661	25,382

ASSETS JANE JONES	1997	1998	1999	2000	2001	2002
Cash in bank	10,000	10,400	10,816	11,249	11,699	12,167
C.S.B.'s/GIC's	20,000	20,800	21,632	22,497	23,397	24,333
Cash Equivalents	5,000	5,200	5,408	5,624	5,849	6,083
INVESTMENT OF SURPLUS CASH	9,941	21,386	34,970	50,460	67,835	87,308
Equities	20,000	22,000	24,200	26,620	29,282	32,210
Mutual Funds	40,000	44,000	48,400	53,240	58,564	64,420
RRSP's						
—Term deposits/Cash equiv	2,000	2,200	2,420	2,662	2,928	3,221
—Bonds/fixed income	50,000	55,000	60,500	66,550	73,205	80,526
—Mutual funds—CDN	75,000	96,000	119,100	144,510	172,461	203,207
—Mutual funds—Foreign	23,000	25,300	27,830	30,613	33,674	37,042
—Mutual funds—Other	10,000	11,000	12,100	13,310	14,641	16,105
RESP	5,000	5,500	6,050	1,655	(3,180)	(13,497)
				40,000	40,000	40,000
SUB-TOTAL LIQUID ASSETS	269,941	318,786	373,426	468,990	530,355	593,125
Pension Plan Value	0	0	0	0	0	0
Limited partnerships	50,000	50,000	50,000	50,000	50,000	50,000
Principal residence (50%)	100,000	104,000	108,160	112,486	116,986	121,665
Cottage (50%)	50,000	52,000	54,080	56,243	58,493	60,833
Other personal assets	5,000	5,200	5,408	5,624	5,849	6,083
SUB-TOTAL LONG-TERM ASSETS	205,000	211,200	217,648	224,353	231,328	238,581
BUSINESS ASSETS						
Shares in small business:						
Jane Jones—Inc.	50,000	60,000	72,000	86,400	103,680	124,416
SUB-TOTAL BUSINESS ASSETS	50,000	60,000	72,000	86,400	103,680	124,416
TOTAL ASSETS	524,941	589,986	663,074	779,743	865,363	956,122
LIABILITIES	10,000	10,000	10,000	10,000	10,000	10,000
TOTAL LIABILITIES	10,000	10,000	10,000	10,000	10,000	10,000
TOTAL NET WORTH	514,941	579,986	653,074	769,743	855,363	946,122

appendix 3

ASSETS BILL SMITH	1997	1998	1999	2000	2001	2002
Cash in bank	10,000	10,400	10,816	11,249	11,699	12,167
C.S.B.'s/Savings Accounts	20,000	20,800	21,632	22,497	23,397	24,333
INVESTMENT OF SURPLUS CASH	9,941	21,386	34,970	50,460	67,835	87,308
RRSP's						
—Term deposits	2,000	2,200	2,420	2,662	2,928	3,221
—Bonds/fixed income	30,000	33,000	36,300	39,930	43,923	48,315
—Mutual funds—CDN	50,000	68,500	88,850	111,235	135,859	162,944
—Mutual funds—Foreign	5,000	5,500	6,050	6,655	7,321	8,053
—Mutual funds—Other	5,000	5,500	6,050	6,655	7,321	8,053
RESP	10,000	11,000	12,100	8,310	(859)	(5,945)
SUB-TOTAL LIQUID ASSETS	141,941	178,286	219,188	259,653	299,424	348,449
Pension Plan Value	0	0	0	0	0	0
Limited partnerships						
Principal residence (50%)	100,000	104,000	108,160	112,486	116,986	121,665
Cottage (50%)	50,000	52,000	54,080	56,243	58,493	60,833
Other personal assets	20,000	20,800	21,632	22,497	23,397	24,333
SUB-TOTAL LONG-TERM ASSETS	170,000	176,800	183,872	191,226	198,876	206,831
BUSINESS ASSETS						
Shares in small business:	0	0	0	0	0	0
SUB-TOTAL BUSINESS ASSETS	0	0	0	0	0	0
TOTAL ASSETS	311,941	355,086	403,060	450,879	498,300	555,280
LIABILITIES	5,000	5,000	5,000	5,000	5,000	5,000
TOTAL LIABILITIES	5,000	5,000	5,000	5,000	5,000	5,000
TOTAL NET WORTH	306,941	350,086	398,060	445,879	493,300	550,280

COMBINED	1997	1998	1999	2000	2001	2002
Cash in bank	20,000	20,800	21,632	22,497	23,397	24,333
C.S.B.'s	40,000	41,600	43,264	44,995	46,974	48,666
Cash Equivalents	5,000	5,200	5,408	5,624	5,849	6,083
INVESTMENT OF SURPLUS CASH	19,882	42,771	69,939	100,919	135,669	174,616
Equities	20,000	22,000	24,200	26,620	29,282	32,210
Mutual Funds	40,000	44,000	48,400	56,240	58,564	64,420
RRSP's						
—Term deposits/Cash equiv.	4,000	4,400	4,840	5,324	5,856	6,442
—Bonds/fixed income	80,000	88,000	96,800	106,480	117,128	128,841
—Mutual funds—CDN	125,000	164,500	207,950	255,745	308,320	366,151
—Mutual funds—Foreign	28,000	30,800	33,880	37,268	40,995	45,094
—Mutual funds—Other	15,000	16,500	18,150	19,965	21,962	24,158
RESP	15,000	16,500	18,150	9,965	(859)	(5,945)
	0	0	0	40,000	40.000	40,000
SUB-TOTAL LIQUID ASSETS	411,882	497,071	592,613	731,642	833,137	955,069
Pension Plan Value	0	0	0	0	0	0
Limited partnerships	50,000	50,000	50,000	50,000	50,000	50,000
Principal residence	200,000	208,000	216,320	224,973	233,972	243,331
Cottage	100,000	104,000	108,160	112,486	116,986	121,665
Other personal assets	25,000	26,000	27,040	28,122	29,246	30,416
SUB-TOTAL LONG-TERM ASSETS	375,000	388,000	401,520	415,581	430,204	445,412
BUSINESS ASSETS						
Shares in small business:	50,000	60,000	72,000	86,400	103,680	124,416
SUB-TOTAL BUSINESS ASSETS	50,000	60,000	72,000	86,400	103,680	124,416
TOTAL ASSETS	836,882	945,071	1,066,133	1,233,623	1,367,021	1,524,897
LIABILITIES	15,000	15,000	15,000	15,000	15,000	15,000
TOTAL LIABILITIES	15,000	15,000	15,000	15,000	15,000	15,000
TOTAL NET WORTH	821,882	930,071	1,051,133	1,218,623	1,352,021	1,509,897

appendix 4
business plan

These work sheets are an illustration of the financial elements of a good business plan. These must be supported by a list of assumptions and all the elements mentioned in Chapter 5.

BASIC ASSUMPTIONS

1. Living expenses increase at 2% per year
2. Cash, Savings accounts at 4% return
3. Other investments 10% return
4. House and cottage value grows at 4% per year
5. Investment of surplus cash makes 10% per year
6. Jane will take a salary of $100,000 per year from business
7. Bill earns a salary of $75,000 from his job and $25,000 from Jane's business
8. Jane's business has an estimated value of $50,000 which is expected to grow at 20% per year
9. Basic RRSP maximum will not change over the next 5 years
10. Surplus cash split 50–50
11. Only current liabilities—no mortgage or other debt

Jane Jones Manufacturing Inc.
Budgeted Balance Sheet
For the Year Ended September 30, 1998

	OCT 97	NOV 97	DEC 97	JAN 98	FEB 98	MAR 98	APR 98	MAY 98	JUN 98	JUL 98	AUG 98	SEP 98
ASSETS												
CURRENT												
Accounts Receivable	72,800	101,600	122,533	136,489	151,793	159,995	167,463	172,442	177,761	181,308	189,672	195,248
Inventory	74,000	92,000	96,000	98,000	101,000	106,000	114,000	122,000	108,000	94,000	88,000	80,000
Prepaids	7,500	7,500	7,500	7,500	7,500	7,500	7,500	7,500	7,500	7,500	7,500	7,500
TOTAL CURRENT ASSETS	154,300	201,100	226,033	241,989	260,293	273,495	288,963	301,942	293,261	282,808	285,172	282,748
CAPITAL	61,500	60,500	59,500	58,500	57,500	56,500	55,500	54,500	53,500	52,500	51,500	50,500
TOTAL ASSETS	**215,800**	**261,600**	**285,533**	**300,489**	**317,793**	**329,995**	**344,463**	**356,442**	**346,761**	**335,308**	**336,672**	**333,248**
LIABILITIES & EQUITY												
CURRENT												
Bank Loan	13,600	44,200	78,933	86,689	89,793	92,795	93,063	95,842	96,961	86,308	74,472	61,248
Accounts Payable	90,000	100,000	90,000	100,000	115,000	125,000	140,000	150,000	140,000	140,000	150,000	160,000
Income Tax	4,586	6,012	6,058	5,644	5,690	5,736	5,782	5,828	5,874	5,920	6,886	7,070
Term Loan	49,000	48,000	47,000	46,000	45,000	44,000	43,000	42,000	41,000	40,000	39,000	38,000
TOTAL LIABILITIES	157,186	198,212	221,991	238,333	255,483	267,531	281,845	293,670	283,835	272,228	270,358	266,318
Common Stock	—	—	—	—	—	—	—	—	—	—	—	—
Retained Earnings	58,613	63,387	63,541	62,155	62,309	62,463	62,617	62,771	62,925	63,079	66,313	66,929
TOTAL EQUITY	58,614	63,388	63,542	62,156	62,310	62,464	62,618	62,772	62,926	63,080	66,314	66,930
TOTAL LIABS & EQUITY	**215,800**	**261,600**	**285,533**	**300,489**	**317,793**	**329,995**	**344,463**	**356,442**	**346,761**	**335,308**	**336,672**	**333,248**
	0	0	0	0	0	0	0	0	0	0	0	0

Jane Jones Manufacturing Inc.
Budgeted Income Statement
For the Year Ended September 30, 1998

	OCT 97	NOV 97	DEC 97	JAN 98	FEB 98	MAR 98	APR 98	MAY 98	JUN 98	JUL 98	AUG 98	SEP 98	TOTAL
SALES	53,000	67,000	55,000	55,000	61,000	59,000	61,000	61,000	63,000	63,000	69,000	69,000	736,000
COST OF SALES	36,000	42,000	36,000	38,000	42,000	40,000	42,000	42,000	44,000	44,000	46,000	48,000	500,000
GROSS PROFIT —$	17,000	25,000	19,000	17,000	19,000	19,000	19,000	19,000	19,000	19,000	23,000	21,000	236,000
—%	32.08%	37.31%	34.55%	30.91%	31.15%	32.20%	31.15%	31.15%	30.16%	30.16%	33.33%	30.43%	32.07%
SELLING & ADMIN EXPENSES													
Salary/Commission	2,500	2,500	2,500	2,500	2,500	2,500	2,500	2,500	2,500	2,500	2,500	2,500	30,000
Salary—Jane	8,300	8,300	8,300	8,300	8,300	8,300	8,300	8,300	8,300	8,300	8,300	8,700	100,000
Salary—Bill	2,000	2,000	2,000	2,000	2,000	2,000	2,000	2,000	2,000	2,000	2,000	3,000	25,000
Benefits	1,250	1,250	1,250	1,250	1,250	1,250	1,250	1,250	1,250	1,250	1,250	1,250	15,000
Employee Expense	175	175	175	175	175	175	175	175	175	175	175	175	2,100
Supplies	200	200	200	200	200	200	200	200	200	200	200	200	2,400
Communication	300	300	300	300	300	300	300	300	300	300	300	300	3,600
Freight-Out	100	100	100	100	100	100	100	100	100	100	100	100	1,200
Repairs	500	500	500	500	500	500	500	500	500	500	500	500	6,000
Rentals	200	200	200	200	200	200	200	200	200	200	200	200	2,400
Insurance & Taxes	300	300	300	300	300	300	300	300	300	300	300	300	3,600
Promotion	200	200	200	200	200	200	200	200	200	200	200	200	2,400
Prof Service	400	400	400	400	400	400	400	400	400	400	400	400	4,800
Utilities	300	300	300	300	300	300	300	300	300	300	300	300	3,600
Bad Debt	200	200	200	200	200	200	200	200	200	200	200	200	2,400
Membership	150	150	150	150	150	150	150	150	150	150	150	150	1,800
Interest	400	400	400	400	400	400	400	400	400	400	400	400	4,800
Miscellaneous	325	325	325	325	325	325	325	325	325	325	325	325	3,900
TOTAL EXPENSES	17,800	17,800	17,800	17,800	17,800	17,800	17,800	17,800	17,800	17,800	17,800	19,200	215,000
Operating Income	(800)	7,200	1,200	(800)	1,200	1,200	1,200	1,200	1,200	1,200	5,200	1,800	21,000
Depreciation	1,000	1,000	1,000	1,000	1,000	1,000	1,000	1,000	1,000	1,000	1,000	1,000	12,000
NET INCOME BEFORE TAX	(1,800)	6,200	200	(1,800)	200	200	200	200	200	200	4,200	800	9,000
Income Tax	(414)	1,426	46	(414)	46	46	46	46	46	46	966	184	2,070
NET INCOME	**(1,386)**	**4,774**	**154**	**(1,386)**	**154**	**154**	**154**	**154**	**154**	**154**	**3,234**	**616**	**6,930**

Jane Jones Manufacturing Inc.
Accounts Receivable
For the Year Ended September 30, 1998

	OCT 97	NOV 97	DEC 97	JAN 98	FEB 98	MAR 98	APR 98	MAY 98	JUN 98	JUL 98	AUG 98	SEP 98	TOTAL
Opening Balance	60,000	72,800	101,600	122,533	136,489	151,793	159,995	167,463	172,442	177,761	181,308	189,672	60,000
ADD: Sales	53,000	67,000	55,000	55,000	61,000	59,000	61,000	61,000	63,000	63,000	69,000	69,000	736,000
LESS:													
Cash Receipts	40,000	38,000	33,867	40,844	45,496	50,598	53,332	55,821	57,481	59,254	60,436	63,224	598,352
Bad Debts	200	200	200	200	200	200	200	200	200	200	200	200	2,400
Closing Balance	**72,800**	**101,600**	**122,533**	**136,489**	**151,793**	**159,995**	**167,463**	**172,442**	**177,761**	**181,308**	**189,672**	**195,248**	**195,248**
Bank Loan Primary Coverage													
Receivables at 75%	54,600	76,200	91,900	102,367	113,844	119,996	125,598	129,332	133,321	135,981	142,254	146,436	
Bank Operating Line	13,600	44,200	78,933	86,689	89,793	92,795	93,063	95,842	96,961	86,308	74,472	61,248	
Coverage	4.01	1.72	1.16	1.18	1.27	1.29	1.35	1.35	1.37	1.58	1.91	2.39	

Inventory
For the Year Ended September 30, 1998

	OCT 97	NOV 97	DEC 97	JAN 98	FEB 98	MAR 98	APR 98	MAY 98	JUN 98	JUL 98	AUG 98	SEP 98	TOTAL
Opening Balance	50,000	74,000	92,000	96,000	98,000	101,000	106,000	114,000	122,000	108,000	94,000	88,000	50,000
ADD: Purchases	60,000	60,000	40,000	40,000	45,000	45,000	50,000	50,000	30,000	30,000	40,000	40,000	530,000
LESS: Cost of Sales	36,000	42,000	36,000	38,000	42,000	40,000	42,000	42,000	44,000	44,000	46,000	48,000	500,000
Closing Balance	**74,000**	**92,000**	**96,000**	**98,000**	**101,000**	**106,000**	**114,000**	**122,000**	**108,000**	**94,000**	**88,000**	**80,000**	**80,000**
Inventory Turnover (days)	45	61	69	71	73	76	80	86	84	74	66	61	47

Jane Jones Manufacturing Inc.
Cash Flow
For the Year Ended September 30, 1998

	OCT 97	NOV 97	DEC 97	JAN 98	FEB 98	MAR 98	APR 98	MAY 98	JUN 98	JUL 98	AUG 98	SEP 98	TOTAL
Opening Cash	(10,000)	(13,600)	(44,200)	(78,933)	(86,689)	(89,793)	(92,795)	(93,063)	(95,842)	(96,961)	(86,308)	(74,472)	(10,000)
Cash Receipts:													
From Receivables	40,000	38,000	33,867	40,844	45,496	50,598	53,332	55,821	57,481	59,254	60,436	63,224	598,352
Cash Disbursements:													
From Operations	17,600	17,600	17,600	17,600	17,600	17,600	17,600	17,600	17,600	17,600	19,000	212,600	212,600
For Inventory	25,000	50,000	50,000	30,000	30,000	35,000	35,000	40,000	40,000	30,000	30,000	30,000	425,000
Term Loan Repay	1,000	1,000	1,000	1,000	1,000	1,000	1,000	1,000	1,000	1,000	1,000	1,000	12,000
Closing Cash	(13,600)	(44,200)	(78,933)	(86,689)	(89,793)	(92,795)	(93,063)	(95,842)	(96,961)	(86,308)	(74,472)	(61,248)	(61,248)

Accounts Payable
For the Year Ended September 30, 1998

	OCT 97	NOV 97	DEC 97	JAN 98	FEB 98	MAR 98	APR 98	MAY 98	JUN 98	JUL 98	AUG 98	SEP 98	TOTAL
Opening Balance	55,000	90,000	100,000	90,000	100,000	115,000	125,000	140,000	150,000	140,000	140,000	150,000	55,000
ADD:													
Purchase Inventory	60,000	60,000	40,000	40,000	45,000	45,000	50,000	50,000	30,000	30,000	40,000	40,000	530,000
Operating Expenses	17,600	17,600	17,600	17,600	17,600	17,600	17,600	17,600	17,600	17,600	17,600	19,000	212,600
LESS:													
Inventory Payments	25,000	50,000	50,000	30,000	30,000	35,000	35,000	40,000	40,000	30,000	30,000	30,000	425,000
Operating Expense	17,600	17,600	17,600	17,600	17,600	17,600	17,600	17,600	17,600	17,600	17,600	19,000	212,600
Closing Balance	90,000	100,000	90,000	100,000	115,000	125,000	140,000	140,000	140,000	140,000	150,000	160,000	160,000

index